Where Everybody Knows Your Name

Best Practices in the Small Church

Marilyn Johns

Copyright Page

Copyright © 2013 by Marilyn Johns

First Published in the United States by:

VTS Press
3737 Seminary Road
Alexandria, VA 22304
www.vts.edu

Edited by
Isabella Blanchard

Cover Design by
Thomas Zdancewiz

ISBN
978-0615851884
0615851886
Printed in the United States of America
Publication date August 2013
First Edition

Where Everybody Knows Your Name

Best Practices in the Small Church

Contents

INTRODUCTION
    1

    The Summer Collegium Project

    Learnings

    Making Connections

    Best Practices

    Purpose of This Book and Acknowledgements

CHAPTER ONE: WHAT ARE SMALL CHURCHES, AND HOW DID THEY GET THAT WAY?
    11

    Definition of a Small Church

    Current Data on Small Churches

    How Churches Become Small

    Context of Ministry

    History

    Discovering Your Church's Identity

CHAPTER TWO: THE VALUE OF SMALL CONGREGATIONS
    24

    Church Growth vs. Church Health

    Small Church Esteem

    Planning and Appreciative Inquiry

    Clergy and the Small Church

CHAPTER THREE: PROCLAIMING THE GOOD NEWS – WORSHIP AND PREACHING
38

If We Just Got a Rock Band, We'd Attract Young People

Authentic and Relevant Worship

Innovative Worship

Music and Music Styles

Making Changes in Worship – Proceed with Caution!

Accessible Worship

CHAPTER FOUR: TELLING THE STORY – CHRISTIAN EDUCATION
54

They Gave Us Permission to Think Outside the Box!

Children's Ministry

Youth Ministry

Adult Ministry

New Ways of Looking at Christian Education

CHAPTER FIVE: INSIDE THE WALLS – CARING FOR SELF AND CONGREGATION
76

Pastoral Care

Care of the Pastor by the Congregation

Care of the Pastor by the Pastor

Care of Volunteers

The Value of Funerals and Baptisms

CHAPTER SIX: OUTSIDE THE WALLS – MISSION AND OUTREACH
92

Can We Make a Difference?

Understanding the Context of Ministry for Mission

Ecumenical and Integrated Ministry

Welcoming the Stranger

Getting Outside the Walls

CHAPTER SEVEN: PASTOR AND PEOPLE – LEADERSHIP
109

Leadership in Family and Pastoral Churches

The Pastor Shouldn't Be the First One at the Church on Sunday Morning: Lay Leadership in the Small Church

Equipping and Supporting Lay Leaders

The Importance of Spiritual Leadership

Stewardship and Other Unpleasant Subjects

CHAPTER EIGHT: THE FUTURE OF THE SMALL CHURCH
132

Envisioning the Future of Your Church

The Changing Role of Clergy

Leaving a Legacy

What Can Denominations Do to Support Small Congregations?

What Can Seminaries Do to Support Small Congregations?

Can Small Churches Survive?

ENDNOTES
152

INTRODUCTION

This book grew out of my experience for six years with the Summer Collegium, a Lilly Endowment-funded project in their "Making Connections" initiative. When Lilly solicited proposals from seminaries, forward thinking people at Virginia Theological Seminary, notably the Rev. Dr. Roger A. Ferlo, the Very Rev. Martha J. Horne, and the Rev. Dr. J. Barney Hawkins, put their heads together and decided to focus their proposal on small congregations. They were clear from the beginning that their focus was to be on celebrating and appreciating the ministry of congregations whose average Sunday attendance was below 100, rather than on pushing small churches to grow. I am very grateful for this emphasis, and believe this is the most effective way to transform small congregations into vital, healthy places of worship and service. Much of the literature and denominational emphasis related to small congregations focuses on numbers, and understandably so. Denominations are shrinking. "How to" books sell. Through the Summer Collegium project we have been affirmed in our thesis that small churches are much more than numbers, to coin a phrase from Loren Mead. These congregations are places of connection, care, mission, and worship for faithful souls, many of whom have been a part of the same congregation for most of their lives.

The Summer Collegium Project

The vision for the Summer Collegium was to connect small church clergy, along with their spouses or partners, with the resources of the Seminary, and also with one another. The project was designed to be ecumenical; in fact, I was hired to manage the project specifically because I was not part of the Episcopal tradition, as Virginia Theological Seminary (VTS) is. For each of the five years of the project we welcomed 25 clergy, about 18 spouses or partners, and nearly 25 leaders and teachers.

Participants were chosen through a rigorous application process in which the pastor, spouse, and someone from the governing board of the church answered several narrative questions, and included a reference. A team of readers was chosen to evaluate the applications, and along with my evaluations of each application participants were selected. We looked for healthy congregations, healthy clergy, healthy relationships, unique ministry, experience in ministry, and an indication that they would take what they learned during their time at VTS back to their congregations and their denominations. After all of those factors were considered, we used demographic information, including geographic location, denomination, gender, and age, to narrow the field to a diverse group of 25.

We gave participants some homework to do before they came. Clergy were required to do some kind of congregational study with their members, usually a time line. They had a book or two to read (spouses and partners got their own copies) and discuss with their council. They were asked to write a case study using a recent incident in their congregation in which they were a key player, using behavioral and theological reflection to evaluate the case. The case studies were a favorite of clergy participants. While they were at the Collegium they presented their cases in small groups and, using the method popular in VTS's Doctor of Ministry program, had to sit silently while the group discussed the case.

The nine-day on-campus time was filled with keynote speakers (among them, Carl Dudley, Anthony Pappas, and Alice Mann) and workshops centered around a particular theme for the year – Mission and Outreach, Christian Education, Worship and Preaching, Clergy Wholeness, and Leadership. There were multiple opportunities for worship each day, and we tried to build in free time for reflection and rest. Participants were also given time to see some of the nation's capital and we took them to a theater event each year. While the spouses and partners were at VTS (the first four days) we housed them in the Hilton Alexandria Mark Center hotel, a luxury hotel near the campus. They were bused to the Washington National Cathedral for worship on Sunday. The hope was to give them some time for retreat and contemplation in a setting that provided comfort and a bit more.

In the year following the Summer Collegium, follow-up visits were made to each of the congregations. The reason for the visits was to engage the congregation in the project, so that it was not only the clergy (and spouse/partner) who participated, but church members and friends as well. The "typical" visit consisted of some kind of workshop, either for the congregation or for neighboring churches or denominational bodies, or any combination of these, a sermon on Sunday, and some sightseeing in the area.

A primary goal of the Summer Collegium was to keep small-church pastors engaged in active ministry for the long term, by

- Providing spiritual resources to small-church clergy and their spouses or partners in a comfortable, retreat-like setting, with all expenses paid.

- Nurturing and strengthening clergy household

- Developing new leadership skills for clergy in small congregations, and following up with lay leaders in participants' own parishes

- Developing new ecumenical strategies for networking and mentoring

- Exploring new directions in worship and music for small congregations

- Recommending and demonstrating appropriate computer technology for those engaged in small church work

- Providing resources for continuing education, including distance learning, and cultural enrichment

- Celebrating the creativity and stability of small church life

Learnings

While the Summer Collegium was not a research project per se, there were many things we either learned or confirmed through its life. You will see these incorporated into the chapters of this book.

Ecumenism

One of our primary learnings was that ecumenical ministry works. Every year participants asked me how we got a group that was so well-suited to one another, and the truth is, there is grace. We have welcomed folks from fairly conservative churches and those from more liberal ones. We have welcomed people of many different ethnic groups and ages. Almost without exception, participants have gotten along well with each other. The issues around ministry in the small church are not bound by theological, denominational, or demographic parameters. A small-town African-American congregation in the Missionary Baptist tradition has many of the same joys and concerns as a progressive Caucasian Lutheran church in the city. Our similarities are much greater than our differences.

Spouses and Partners

Another area we felt strongly about in this project was the inclusion of spouses and partners. This did not come easily. Every year there were applications from clergy who said their spouses didn't participate in any way in their church, so they didn't want to come. Or they had to work. We held our ground, believing that the primary source of support for a small-church pastor is the person with whom he/she lives in a committed relationship. The spouses and partners who attended affirmed this every year. There is a difference in hearing someone tell you about an event and experiencing it for yourself. Couples were grateful for time away to reflect on their ministry. Spouses/partners appreciated hearing the keynote speakers talk about the small church in ways they could recognize and relate to. We thought that this would be the case when it was written into the grant, but it was affirmed over and over by participants.

Not surprisingly, we fielded a fair amount of criticism over including partners in the project. Each year there were phone calls asking me to clarify what a "partner" was, which usually ended with a sure judgment that my soul was in grave danger. Any time an event is planned to include clergy and their significant others, and it is an ecumenical project, provision has to be made for those denominations, including the Episcopal Church, the United Church of Canada and United Church of Christ, and now the ELCA and Presbyterian churches, that are accepting of same-sex couples and couples in long-term committed relationships. We were up front about this in our publicity, and the people who applied did so knowing that this was the case. One heterosexual couple said, "If you had not included partners, we would not have applied." We never had any issues of disrespect or even blatant discomfort among our participants, even though I know some did not accept that lifestyle.

With the inclusion of spouses and partners, we learned that the role of the significant other in a clergy relationship is changing. The first year of the project (2006) there were many applications in which the female spouse said, "My role in the church is the typical role of a pastor's wife: I gather the ladies' group, I teach Sunday School, I play piano, and I host a luncheon at our home every year at Christmastime." The male spouses in that year were a little more vague about their roles. As the years went by, a "typical" male spouse role emerged: "I run the sound system, I maintain the buildings and grounds, and I am in charge of the office computers" became the new role of male spouses. More and more female spouses, on the other hand, did not see their only occupation as pastor's wife; many work outside the home and support the church as any other member would.

Denominational Support

It was confirmed over and over that many small-church pastors do not always feel supported in their call and their ministry by the larger church. This is not surprising given the fact that denominations (and middle governing bodies, like presbyteries, annual conferences, dioceses, and ELCA synods) are struggling to understand their role and their identity, and feeling pressure as they grow smaller themselves. It's a trickle-down situation: middle judicatories are getting pressure for more money and more numbers from the denomination. They pass that angst on to the churches, especially the small churches, some of whom have a hard time giving any financial support to the denomination.

Small Churches are Here to Stay

Carl Dudley talks about small churches as being "tenacious and ubiquitous, but also out of step."[1] Thirty years ago, when the mega-churches were just beginning to be a phenomenon, some thought small churches would all be absorbed into these huge, often non-denominational gatherings.[2] This has not been the case. If anything, the number of small churches has grown in the past 30 years. Small churches are not going away any time soon (look at Chapter 8 for more on this topic).

Small churches are indeed ubiquitous, populating most small towns in America and Canada, and many cities. Estimates from mainline U.S. and Canadian denominations report between 70% and 80% of their churches worshiping fewer than 100 on an average Sunday, although we sometimes look at large church buildings and think they are large congregations. During the church boom of the 1950s and 1960s churches were built in towns all over the country, anticipating (and sometimes experiencing) full pews. If you visit small towns in Middle America, you are likely to find six or seven churches – one each of ELCA, United Methodist, Episcopalian, Presbyterian, at least one kind of Baptist, perhaps a United Church of Christ and Disciples of Christ. In addition there is usually a Roman Catholic church and a Pentecostal church. When a town has lost its major industry and is down to 1000 people, it doesn't take a math major to figure out that all of these congregations are small. There may be one large non-denominational church in town which the other churches bemoan "they're stealing all our children" because their size allows them to offer full education and youth programs.

The "out of step" aspect of small congregations refers to the fact that small churches are counter-cultural. In a culture of "bigger is better" and "the one with the most toys wins," small churches are simple and more interested in relationships than large numbers. Healthy small congregations are learning that they don't have to try to be all things to all people, but should focus in on a few ministries they are passionate about, and work to make those excellent.

Making Connections

One of the primary purposes for the Summer Collegium, and the reason the Lilly Endowment invested in this project, was to explore new ways of making connections. This was accomplished with the Collegium in a number of different ways.

- Clergy connecting with the Seminary. Many of the Summer Collegium participants live in remote areas of the country (and Canada) and are not in a position to utilize the resources of a seminary. By bringing them to Virginia we allowed them to experience residential campus life again – and for some locally ordained persons, this may have been the first time. Clergy and spouses/partners were given a library card to the Bishop Payne Library, which was good for a year (the library will mail items).

- Clergy and spouses/partners connecting with one another. Nine days away from responsibilities for church, family, jobs, and life-as-usual was a welcome break for couples and singles. There was plenty of free time to explore the city together and just talk to each other uninterrupted. For the first four nights, participants were housed in a nice hotel, a luxury some could not otherwise afford.

- Clergy connecting with other clergy. This was noticed most profoundly during the case study sessions, where groups of five clergy and two facilitators discussed a situation that had occurred recently in each of their respective churches. Many clergy are part of lectionary study groups and some are part of cluster groups in their denomination, but it is not often that they are able to get an objective view of something without fearing a breach of confidentiality or embarrassment that might be present in a local group. Some of the participant case study groups have continued this practice when needed, sharing a particularly difficult situation with their group of colleagues from other denominations and other parts of the country. In addition to the case study groups, there was also a good bit of general sharing during mealtimes together.

- Spouses and partners connecting with other spouses and partners. Most mid-level councils do not provide support for partners of clergy. Some spouse groups have formed through the efforts of individual spouses and partners, but in most cases they just don't exist. The role of spouse/partner can be very lonely – they are members of the church, but don't have a pastor; they get blamed for things the pastor does that upset someone; they are asked to be message carriers to the pastor; they are not usually allowed to serve on the church's board, nor are they comfortable doing so if it is permissible. The spouse/partner participants of the Summer Collegium came eager to connect with others who share their role.

- The Seminary and the project connecting with congregations. The follow-up visits went a long way toward making this connection. Church members were able to hear a word of hope about their situation and their congregation. For many congregations with low self-esteem, hearing that their pastor and their congregation were chosen from a large pool of applicants made them sit up just a little bit straighter. Many times the only thing they hear from outsiders is the denomination pressuring them to grow. Having someone, a stranger, come in with no hidden agenda and give them some tools to think in positive ways about their ministry was helpful. The visitor was often able to make suggestions or point out assets, perhaps using the same words the pastor had been using for years, but members heard them differently from this objective outsider.

- Sharing the connections with those who did not attend the summer conferences. Throughout the program, we encouraged those who participated to share the experiences with their denominations, with other clergy in their towns, and with friends and colleagues all over the countries. This has happened in many, many places. Alumni of the Summer Collegium have led workshops in their regions, some have had newspaper articles published about their experience, all have shared it with their congregations. In addition, we were able to start a small church ministry e-newsletter which reached hundreds of small church pastors and members all over the U.S. and Canada. Virginia Seminary has also made videos of many of the keynotes and workshops from the five years of the Collegium available at no charge for download on their website, www.vts.edu/smallchurches.

- Continuing connections. Many of the connections made in nine days in Virginia continue to this day, mostly through Facebook. Some participants have visited one another, or met at a halfway point for dinner. For the year following their summer experience, each spouse/partner and clergy person received a birthday card. Prayer requests are often sent to the colleague group, such as when one town was flooding, when a spouse died unexpectedly, and when a pastoral transition was occurring.

Best Practices

In visiting nearly 125 small congregations during the five-year period of the grant, I was profoundly impressed by the ministry that goes on in places with 35 people on an average Sunday. The stereotypical version of a small church filled with older people who have no energy and no interest in welcoming others or doing mission is out there, but the congregations and clergy we encountered in this project were largely people of hope and love for God and for one another. They were eager to try new things, open to new ideas, and excited about ministry. And boy can they cook! I shudder to think of the number of potlucks I have attended in churches all over North America over the past five years!

There are lots of innovative ideas being tried in these congregations, and many of their people want to learn and grow spiritually. They love being small, and would not want to get so large that they lose the close relationships they have with one another.

Through the course of this book we will encounter a number of small congregations across the U.S. and Canada. As I say to many congregations, it's not about numbers, it's about faithfulness; it's not about being like the big churches, it's about using the gifts we have been given by God to the glory of God's kingdom.

Purpose of This Book and Acknowledgements

We have had a unique opportunity to share the generosity of the Lilly Endowment with small congregations in a way that has changed lives, changed pastorates, and changed attitudes about the small church. The purpose of writing this all down is to share it with those small congregations who were not part of the project – not to give you a "how-to" manual for being a strong, healthy small congregation, but to perhaps inspire you to try new things with boldness, to appreciate who you are as a small church, and to celebrate your smallness.

This project changed my life. Before I learned about the Summer Collegium project I was working as a Director of Christian Education in a program-sized church. Although I was a member of a small church, I was not an active part of it, as I was engaged in another church on Sundays. I had been having a bit of a personal faith crisis as I read all the literature about mega-churches, and being distressed by it. I remember thinking, "If this is the future of the church, maybe I should think about working in a secular setting." I didn't really learn about small churches until I was presented with the grant proposal. After reading it, my first thought was, "This is what church is supposed to be about!" That assessment has not changed.

This book could not have been completed without the help and encouragement of friends and colleagues who helped along the way: Roger Ferlo and Barney Hawkins, the original Project Directors; Martha Horne, who helped in the visioning of the project and was a warm and welcoming presence as the Dean and President of Virginia Seminary; the current Dean and President of VTS, Ian Markham, who resurrected this book project after a number of transitions left it untouched; and his assistant, Isabella Blanchard, who provided excellent editing suggestions; Joyce Ann Mercer, Kathleen Henderson Staudt, and everyone in the Institute for Christian Formation & Leadership (ICFL) who have been encouragers, colleagues, and friends; and especially my assistant, Maggie Riley, whose help was invaluable in gathering stories from the congregations and jogging my memory. I could not have completed this book without the encouragement of my family and friends, with those "So, how's that book coming?" questions. Thank you all!

I am deeply grateful to the clergy, spouses, partners, and congregations of the close to 150 small churches directly affected by this project. Some pastors have moved on to other churches (usually other small churches!); many are still in ministry in their Summer Collegium churches. Some of you will recognize your churches in the examples given. Thanks also to the several hundred others who applied for a place in the Summer Collegium but were not selected. I wish we could have taken all of you and shared this gift with you. I hope this book will help a little.

1

WHAT ARE SMALL CHURCHES, AND HOW DID THEY GET THAT WAY?

Definition of a Small Church

In putting together an ecumenical project on the small church, we learned quickly that membership numbers are irrelevant and confusing in defining a small congregation. Each denomination has a different way of counting members (some count all baptized members, some only count those who have made a profession of faith, some churches' membership roles include everyone who has ever stepped through their doors). The better indicator is average worship attendance (or some would say ASA, or average Sunday attendance), but that is also getting murky as so many congregations are beginning to offer worship at alternative times. Many are now using 'Regularly Participating Adults' as the standard. For our purposes, we are generally talking about churches with a total worship attendance of 100 or fewer in an average week. In most denominations this translates to about 50 to 200 people on the rolls, but again, use caution. Many ELCA churches, for example, show 400 on the rolls and 75 in worship, simply because they count differently. The focus is less on numbers, and more on how a church functions.

Back in 1983 Arlin Rothauge published a little pamphlet for the Episcopal Church meant to help congregations with their outreach and membership, called "Sizing Up a Congregation for New Member Ministry".[3] In doing so, he effectively changed the language of the church by his then astounding discovery that churches of different sizes actually function differently. So, it's true – small churches are not just like miniature large churches! We in the small church already knew this, of course, but it was nice to hear someone else say it.

Rothauge put congregations into four categories by size: family churches, pastoral churches, program churches, and corporate churches. Since he first pioneered this radical idea, numerous writers and sociologists have expanded on his categories by more fully describing the functioning of the different categories, thus moving away from looking only at numbers. Others have added categories to help describe that awkward period between being a pastoral and a program church. Still others have written about transitions from one category to another.

It is all very helpful, and people in small congregations are often surprised to hear their situations described so accurately. Essentially, the categories of church function are:

- **Family** – Rothauge describes this numerically as 0-50 people "active and attending worship with some regularity",[4] but your congregation may be larger and still function as a family church. A family church is a small, tightly-knit group; often one or two biological families make up the majority of adherents. Even if they are not blood-related, they often function like a family. They have deep love for one another, but can fight like cats and dogs – however, by the next Sunday things are usually fine because, after all, they're family! Dudley describes this church as a single cell of caring – that is, everything that happens involves everyone there.[5] There are usually not groupings by age or gender because it would break up the family. When one hurts, they all hurt, and when one celebrates, they're all invited to the party. It's not easy to become part of a family church; you are either born into it, or adopted in, which means you must be accepted by the existing group. Many family churches have a strong matriarch or patriarch through whom all decision-making must pass, even if that person does not sit on the council. You can't decide to change the color of the walls in the sanctuary without checking with Mabel first. Now, Mabel may have gone on to her reward 20 years ago, but she is still consulted ("What do you think Mabel would have thought of robin's egg blue?"). Many of the matriarchs and patriarchs are benevolent rulers, and may not even realize they hold the power they do, but everyone else knows it, and the pastor had better find out quickly. Clergy in a family church are there for the things it is perceived that only clergy can do: preaching, pastoral care, funerals, leading the Bible study, and administering the sacraments. Any new initiatives come from the people, and they are resistant to ideas from a pastor who will probably only be there for a short time because he/she is either a brand new pastor (who will doubtless leave in search of a larger church soon) or a retired pastor (who wants one more call before hanging it up for good). The attitude is, "We've been here since long before you came, and we'll be here long after you leave, so we'll tolerate you while you're here, but don't expect us to change too much."

> **From the young American Baptist pastor of a congregation in Vermont: You know what I love? I love having dinner with people. Meeting at a coffee shop. Going to see the kids act in the second grade class play. Snowshoeing behind Doug Wright's farm. Getting to know people intimately. Knowing how their house smells in winter. I love small church because every Sunday I climb into that pulpit and know the story of those folks staring back at me.**

- Pastoral - According to Rothauge, the pastoral church has about 50-150 active members,[6] which pushes the boundary of our numerical definition of a small church. A pastoral church is still a single-cell organization, but the cell is larger. The pastoral church is so named because of its increased dependence on the pastor. While in a family church the pastor is merely an appendage, those in the pastoral church depend on the clergy person as their leader. The pastor has a personal relationship with everyone in the congregation, and is the one to visit sick and shut-in members. The pastor is expected to keep everything moving on time, and keep everyone working together. Few visitors return if they cannot relate to the pastor or priest. Members in a pastoral church usually get along well with the pastor and are open to the ideas she brings. Pastoral churches may have some programs and groups, perhaps a Sunday school, a choir, or a women's circle, but they prefer being together over being segregated in groups. The size and growth potential of a pastoral church often depends on how many relationships can be established and maintained by the pastor. You can see how easy it would be for a pastor to be overwhelmed in a pastoral church, and how easy it might be to succumb to the perception that "they need me to get anything done around here." Both of these are dangerous situations that can lead to unhealthy behaviors.

> **The pastor of a Disciples of Christ church in Texas writes: There are so many things that need to be done, and I am responsible for all of them, and I often feel that I am not giving any of them the time and attention they need and deserve. We are blessed to have a couple of dedicated and gifted part-time staff members (a minister of music and a youth director), but on a day-to-day basis, I am usually the only person in the church building – and that can get lonely.**

- Program – The program church, which Rothauge describes as between 150 and 350 persons actively engaged in ministry[7], has more staff, more programs and more groupings than smaller churches do. This type of congregation plays the interesting dual role of being the church many remember from their childhood in the 1950s and 1960s, and therefore the goal to which a small church aspires, and the monster that threatens the family of the small church. In many of the congregations I have visited people look back nostalgically to "the way this church used to be," when the pews were full, there were 200 children in Sunday School (really?), and they merely had to open the doors and visitors would flock in! There were activities at the church every Wednesday and Sunday night, and everyone in town came. Why can't we be that church again? they ask. What are we doing wrong? But then when the church begins to grow and perhaps needs a larger building or two worship services on Sunday, the people resist growing so large that they don't know everyone in church, and they definitely don't want to split the family by adding a worship service. The program church model seems to be the goal and the threat at the same time.

Small congregations generally function as family or pastoral churches, but some, especially those who remember a time when they were larger, try to function as program churches with smaller numbers of people, and a heavy price is paid by members trying to keep up. It is typical, though, for leaders of small churches to recognize characteristics from two or three of Rothauge's categories in their congregations. The lines are always fuzzy, and just because the average Sunday attendance may have gone up to 51 this year does not mean a congregation is automatically going to change its functioning to pastoral style.

The different church functions are important to remember in working with a small congregation because they have a lot to say about the expectations of clergy and of lay people, and how moving from one category to another can have notable, often painful, consequences. Alice Mann gives this topic of size transition a good overview in her book, *The In-Between Church*.[8] A pastor can get understandably frustrated thinking and acting as if she is in a program church, when actually it is a family church, and programming is the last thing the people want to do. Another interesting perspective that Mann offers is that size transition is not a one-way street. Although we may assume size transitions occur when a church grows, in smaller churches the transition may be just as likely to be from larger to smaller. There are confusions and frustrations here, too, and they may be more challenging. Memory plays a big role in understanding the small church, and it is easy for folks to live in the shadow of the church the way it once was.

So, to summarize, some of the ways in which small congregations are unique and may differ from larger congregations, are that they:

- Value intimate relationships.

- Are often populated by people related to one another by birth or marriage.

- Are motivated to keep relationships strong.

- Often have matriarchs and/or patriarchs with a lot of influence.

- Value their history and want to preserve it, for good or for ill.

- Sometimes seem standoffish to outsiders.

- Welcome newcomers in only by birth or adoption, and this process takes awhile.

- Find change to be difficult.

- Love to tell their stories – personal as well as corporate.

- Participate intergenerationally; they don't want to break up the family.

- (In my experience) are innovative, friendly, welcoming, faithful parts of the Body of Christ!

Current Data on Small Churches

There are lots of different numbers floating around about how many people are in small congregations and how many congregations are small. Dudley held on to the 50-15 principle he noted in 1975 that in mainline denominations the smallest 50% of churches served about 15% of the members and the largest 15% of churches served about 50% of the people.[9] I think that this statistic has changed a bit, but some of the data seems contradictory. According to a 2009 study from The Barna Group, 41% of adults attending a Protestant church associate with a congregation of 100 or fewer adults. Only about 9% attend churches of 1000 worshippers or more.[10] At the same time, the National Congregations Study report, American Congregations at the Beginning of the 21st Century, found in both phase one (1998) and phase two (2006-07) of their work, that the average congregation had 75 regular participants, and in both phases the average attendee worshipped in a congregation with about 400 regular participants. Their conclusion mirrors Dudley's: "Most congregations in the United States are small, but most people are in large congregations."[11]

In another study, researchers found that the smallest (attendance 1-49) and largest churches (2000 plus) are growing, while attendance in the middle group is declining. According to this study, between 1994 and 2004 the smallest churches grew 16.4% (national population growth is 12.2%).[12] This suggests that although many people are choosing to join mega-churches, many are also interested in the intimacy that the small church offers. There is room for everyone at the table, whether that table is big, small, or somewhere in between.

How Churches Become Small

When congregations grow, there may be a period of nostalgia, remembering when the pastor could visit every person in the hospital, and on Sunday morning you could greet everyone by name, even noticing who was absent by their empty pew. This nostalgia can cause a pastor to burn out and people to grieve the loss of the "good old days," but it is usually short-lived because they see the upside of the church becoming larger.

When congregations become smaller, however, the nostalgia seems to last much longer. I think this is because it is mixed with feelings of failure and inadequacy. The boom period of the church was in the 1950s and 1960s – that's 50 or 60 years ago – and I still hear congregations lamenting the fact that their present-day Sunday School doesn't have the 200 children that they remember from that boom time. What are we doing wrong? they wonder.

There are a number of reasons small churches are small, and most of them don't have anything to do with doing anything wrong. It is true that some congregations are not welcoming to those outside of the "family," and it is true that in some congregations if a visitor sits in Aunt Tillie's pew, she might ask them to move, but in my experience most small congregations are very open and welcoming to visitors. For a large number of small churches, the reasons they are small fall into one or more of five general categories:

They were once large (often in the 1950s and 1960s), but lost members. Why? There could be a number of factors.

- We are in a Post-Christendom era in this country. It is no longer the norm that everyone in America is Christian and goes to church on Sunday. Sunday is no longer a holy day set aside for church activities. In this country we don't really appreciate the concept of Sabbath. Many Americans and Canadians, and the media, which influences us greatly, see Sunday as a day to sleep in, read the paper, cut the grass, whatever, but usually not go to church. Stores and businesses are open, soccer games (in Canada I am corrected to say 'hockey games') are played, and kids visit their dad in the next town, all on the day that once was reserved for church activities. Take a look at the difference in popular sitcoms of the 50s and today. Ozzie and Harriet went to church with their family; so did Donna Reed. Have you ever seen the characters in "How I Met Your Mother" or "Friends" or even "Modern Family" going to church? Going to church at all in the 21st century is counter-cultural. While there might be some blame to be shared by the church, when there is as radical a cultural shift as there has been in the past sixty years, the church cannot be completely at fault.

- The town or city in which the church is located has fallen on hard economic times; businesses have closed, people have moved away. This is a reality of our culture. When a town was booming in the 1950s because the paper mill had jobs for everyone, new churches were built on every corner of the downtown. It's hard to keep that up after the mill closes. So we're left with small towns all over America and Canada with a population of 600 and eight or nine different churches. Young people who leave don't return because there will not be a job there. Older people who moved there for a job retire in more accessible places.

- Related to this, we are a more mobile society; children move away after college and don't repopulate the church; there isn't the kind of family structure there used to be. There are still many small congregations made up primarily of family members, but this is becoming the exception to the rule. Because of the convenience of travel and the shrinkage of the world, families might be separated by many miles and even countries. If church was once the family gathering place, followed by a big lunch at grandma's house, today we might enjoy a Skype session with a son serving in the army or a daughter teaching in China. If a young person's chances of getting a job are next to none in a small town or rural area, they will not come back to live near family.

- There was some kind of conflict or clergy misconduct that split the church. While I do believe that small churches are less vulnerable to splits over issues than larger churches – keeping the family together usually takes precedence over arguments – they still sometimes happen. Recently, the year after the Evangelical Lutheran Church of America made its decision to allow for the ordination of gays and lesbians, many ELCA small church pastors were worried about a split in their congregations. The same has been the case with the

Episcopal Church and is proving be true for the Presbyterian Church (U.S.A.), as it deals with the consequences of its recent vote. Clergy misconduct can also split churches because there will be some who are badly hurt, and others who want to forgive and be supportive.

They have always been small. In the heyday of the church, many denominations planted churches in every town, and many of these never grew large. By the mid-60s, when the sexual revolution was in full swing and people began to see the church as irrelevant and restricting, church attendance took a big hit. So all of those churches planted in towns across America expecting to be filled experienced a trend in the other direction. They never reached the attendance for which they were built. "If you build it they will come" turned out not be the case in most mainline denominations.

They are new churches, which may or may not quickly grow out of the small church category. Various denominations have had pushes to start new congregations, thinking that unchurched people and young adults are more likely to want to go to a new church rather than an established church. The Disciples of Christ church had that kind of push beginning in 2000, hoping to start 1000 new churches by 2010. The Presbyterian Church (U.S.A.) is beginning such an emphasis now, to be completed in 2020. Many of these new churches will remain small.

They are immigrant churches or "niche" churches. Many of the towns I visited had six or seven evangelical churches, and one progressive church. In a small town, these progressive churches are "niche" churches, established because their founders felt something different was needed in town. Some niche churches are places that openly welcome gay and lesbian people. Some have a strong ethic of social justice. Some are formed around a particular mission. Some form around a particular way of worshipping – a town might have one "low church" Episcopal congregation, and another "high church." In the same way, immigrant communities are establishing congregations all across the country. One difference in immigrant churches and more mainstream churches is that immigrants will drive long distances to go to a church filled with people like themselves. Many of these churches meet in an existing building which they rent from or share with an established congregation, but the two ministries are often completely separate.

They are intentionally small. As hard as you may think that is to believe, some churches really want to be and remain small. If they get to a certain size – usually about 200 members, the point at which it is difficult for everyone to know everyone else – they ask their denomination to plant another church. They don't want to give up the intimacy of the family by starting a second service or expanding their facility. Having said that, some churches sabotage their growth, often without realizing it.

Context of Ministry

It has been interesting to me that over the years of the Summer Collegium project many people have referred to our initiative as a rural ministry project. We've never billed it that way. We have always referred to it as a small church project, but some people naturally equate the small church with rural churches. In the application process, we asked pastors to identify whether their congregations were in rural, small town, suburban, or urban settings. About 1/3 of applicants identified themselves as rural, or they marked both rural and small town. Those identifying as exclusively small town accounted for another 1/3 of applicants. So about 70% of the applicants - and about 60% of those chosen to participate - were from rural or small town settings. The other 30% of applicants were evenly split between suburban churches and urban churches.

There are obvious differences in ministry in a rural or small town setting and a suburban or urban context. In rural areas, church activities must be planned around agricultural activities. During planting season, don't expect to see the men in church much. Don't plan your biggest fundraiser during the harvest, or your workers will be few. In some parts of the country, all community activity, including school, ceases on the first day of deer hunting season. In others, the presence of the county fair will close the schools.

Urban and suburban small churches have a different set of unique circumstances based on their context. Urban congregations often have large, stately, sometimes historic buildings that are mostly empty. The challenge becomes finding ways to best utilize the facility for ministry, and how to pay the heat bills. Many small urban churches get involved in community organizing and advocacy. In suburban churches, many of which were planted in the day when most people walked to church, visibility may become a problem. Does the community know you are there if your church is tucked back in an aging neighborhood? Many urban and suburban churches have to deal with the changing of their communities. What was once the neighborhood with children playing ball in the streets and the local elementary school filled to the brim has now become a neighborhood for empty nesters. Those changes change the church's ministry. In urban areas, it is not uncommon to find an all-white small congregation (usually housed in a big old building) in a predominantly African-American neighborhood. Members drive into the city to go to church, and drive out to go home. Folks in the neighborhood recognize the church as different from themselves, and they stay away.

Knowing the context of ministry is crucial to addressing the needs in your community. Are there ways to include neighborhood residents in the life of your congregation? Is the neighborhood changing, and how will that inform your mission? Do people travel a long distance to get to church, or do they walk? Will they come to the church for evening meetings or Bible studies, or is it a "one-day-a-week" church? What is the racial/ethnic makeup of the community, and is it reflected in the membership of the church? The same question may be asked of age, education, income, and other demographic factors.

History

Each year for the Summer Collegium we asked participants to work with their congregations before the summer session to determine the perceived history of the congregation. Most years we used an exercise from Carl Dudley's book using a congregational timeline.[13] The results were often that the pastor learned more about the church than she had previously known. By looking at the events in the life of the church, superimposed with world events and times member joined, and with pastors who served, a clearer picture of the congregation emerges. Congregational timelines can help to determine how the church became small. Was it a particular incident that split the church, or was it a gradual decline? Did a particular pastor usher in new growth, or did that pastor seem to alienate people? When were the "glory days" of the church, or are they now? What do people remember about particular pastors? Are there some pastors who are not included on the timeline, and was that because of a short tenure or a ministry that was forgettable (or that the people have tried to forget)? How did world history affect the congregation? How did denominational history play a part (we've seen a lot of changes in congregations as a result of votes to ordain women or those in same-sex relationships)? A congregational timeline can be created by getting a roll of butcher paper or newsprint, marking it in decades, and tacking it up around the perimeter of the fellowship hall. Then the people can be gathered for a potluck supper and invited to mark events and pastors, including the time they joined the church. This exercise will generate a lot of discussion and can be fun for everyone.

It is important to note that the memories of church members might not always reflect the facts you might find in the church records – it is significant to note where memory is distorted and what that might indicate. Is this a church that would rather not think about the lean times – do they live in denial? Or do they exaggerate the good times, when there were 50 children in each age-grouped Sunday School class and everyone in the church tithed? What does it mean if they do carry distorted memories? What are the events missing from the timeline; are these things people would rather forget?

Discovering Your Church's Identity

I've learned in my work with small congregations that the healthier churches tend to be aware of how they function and they try to live into their size, rather than longing to be something they are not. They have a good sense of who they are and adjust accordingly to circumstances that arise. This is not to say that a congregation that is negative or depressed is doomed to remain that way; nor does it mean that a healthy church might not succumb to low self-esteem at times.

Congregational timelines are one good way to look at who you are and who you have been as a church. Another way to discover a church's identity is to try and figure out where the congregation's passion lies. Callahan refers to "one excellent mission,"[14] which tries to get at this passion. If a church were to identify what gives the members and visitors energy, and in which activities most people are involved, that might be a clue to what makes this church unique. That one excellent mission becomes the springboard for future activities in the church. For example, if alleviating hunger is the one excellent mission of a congregation, it might get involved in starting a food pantry; it might hang posters that tell about proper nutrition or offer a class for new mothers on making good nutritional choices; it might give out food at Thanksgiving and Christmas to those in need; it might also support a town in Africa that needs seeds and tools to grow crops. The Communion table might be piled high with non-perishable items on the first Sunday of the month, and the bakers in the church might provide a snack for the Vacation Bible School or the preschool that uses their building.

It's about personality; it's about mission; it's about passion.

> **One of my favorite success stories is of a small church in downtown Kansas City, Missouri, that was a merger of three huge congregations that had become small. They made a commitment at the merger to be integrated and remain that way. Years later, they are almost exactly 50% Caucasian and 50% African-American. They get along well with one another, and their identity is formed around their commitment to diversity.**

2

THE VALUE OF THE SMALL CONGREGATION

Why do we bother? Wouldn't it just be easier for all of the small churches to combine together to form medium- to large-sized churches? Isn't the goal to become large? And speaking of large, isn't numerical growth an indication that God is blessing our work? Aren't small churches just a thorn in everyone's side?

If you answered 'yes' to these questions, chances are you have not been part of a small congregation, or, if you have, you did not stay for long. Now don't get me wrong, I'm not ever going to say that all churches should be small, and that large churches are too bureaucratic to be "real" church. I believe churches should come in all sizes. Just as God took great creative license in the formation of humankind, endowing each of us with different gifts, different life circumstances, and different likes and dislikes, so churches have become diverse in their size, their liturgies, their viewpoints, and their activities. There is room for everyone at the table.

Having said that, we in North America live in a society that values big over small. Go to the thesaurus function on the word processing program on your computer and type in "small." The results start out being rather innocuous – little, minute, tiny, diminutive, miniature, petite – but then they get more disparaging – undersized, minor, unimportant, trivial, slight, insignificant, lesser. This is the way many perceive the small church – as unimportant, trivial, depressed, dead or dying. And some are. But many are not.

Church Growth vs. Church Health

In nearly every denomination, there are annual statistical reports that long-suffering board clerks or clergy look forward to like an annual root canal. How many were baptized? How many joined? How many died? What is your net membership gain/loss for the year? What is your annual budget, and how much money went to benevolence and operating costs? Having been a clerk of session in two different Presbyterian Church (USA) churches, I know how much fun these reports can be, especially when I had to guess the age groupings of all the members! The PCUSA and other denominations use these statistics to gauge how well we are doing – and everyone wants to be one of the few congregations that is growing. In the PCUSA, statistics on every individual congregation are published on the website – and they are compared against other PCUSA churches, as in: "Your congregation had 83 members; that is lower than the national average of 227 members. Your budget is lower than the national average…your worship attendance is lower…" Ok, ok, we get it – we're a small church!

In my idea of a perfect church, these annual reports (if we had them at all!) would contain not only bare statistics, questions of quantity, but also questions related to ministry and changed lives. Anyone can add members to their rolls – put a big sign in the front of your church once a month and say, "Free Mercedes to anyone who joins the church today!" I guarantee your numbers will grow. But what will that do to help your ministry? You'll end up with a lot of greedy, self-centered people who don't like to work for what they get. Good luck with that. Instead, what if those reports asked about growth in the number of people who read their Bible every day, or people whose lives have been changed because of your food pantry, or people who gave up their addictions because of the twelve-step groups that meet in your building? What about people whose faith has deepened in the past year, or people who shared their faith with someone else?

To me, those are more accurate signs of health than how many people joined the church. Of course, they are much harder to measure. I think many more small church leaders could give you those kinds of "statistics" than larger church leaders could, though. They know the people as individuals, they know their lives, their relatives, their pets, their joys and sorrows, their vulnerabilities.

I would much rather see a church increase in health than increase in numbers only. Health in the small church is shown in many ways; these will be explored in more depth throughout this book. Generally speaking, a small congregation is healthy if:

- They have a clearly understood mission to love and serve God and neighbor.

- They have a strong outward focus through outreach to the community and missions.

- They are known in their communities for the difference they have made and are making.

- They are reasonably financially stable – able to pay the pastor and keep the lights on.

- They are willing to take some risks and try new things, knowing that not everything will work, but recognizing the value of the trying – "we've always done it that way" is not the rule of the day.

- They have developed healthy ways of dealing with disagreement.

- They have a large percentage of members on the church rolls who are active and involved in the life of the church.

- They recognize that they cannot do everything, and work in partnership with other churches in their community to provide for its needs.

- They enjoy being together; they sing heartily, they stay and talk to each other after the service, they allow themselves to be vulnerable, they are joyful!.

- They appreciate the value of being a small congregation.

The standard by which churches are judged worthy must be changed to include the value of the small congregation.

Small Church Esteem

It is not surprising that the biggest problem facing small churches, as reported by pastors, is negative self-image. Members of small congregations may be tired of trying; the same people seem to do everything; board meetings are a litany of negativity; congregations become complacent, turn upon themselves, and give up. If these symptoms sound familiar, it may be because they are very similar to the symptoms of depression in individuals. Many small churches are depressed.

When we think about healthy self-esteem in individuals, we think of feelings of competence, worth, power, confidence, identity, and joy. When these feelings are missing, a person may be headed for trouble. The same is true in churches, and it can be especially pointed in small churches. Because of all the negative connotations inherent in the idea of being small, these congregations have worries that haunt them – Are we doing something wrong? Is God not blessing us? Are we not valuable enough for God to bless? Low self-esteem manifests itself in the small church by a tendency to listen to those negative voices telling them that they are unworthy, which lowers esteem even more. It can be a deadly cycle: our church is small, we must be doing something wrong, God must not be on our side, we are a failure. The more that attitude prevails, the more it becomes reality as the spoken or unspoken message to visitors is, "Why would you want to come to this church?"

In looking back at the list of reasons a church is small, many of those factors have nothing to do with how faithful a church is in its ministry. Many of the reasons larger churches become small have to do with external factors, such as a cultural shift that makes church-going the exception rather than the rule, the population's tendency to move to cities, the big employer in town moving out, and on and on. The fact that a church is small does not necessarily have anything to do with their doing anything wrong or being unwelcoming or even being unhealthy; it just means that they are living in 21st century America.

So then, what does the small church have to offer that larger churches have to work harder to achieve? First and foremost on the lists of most pastors and members of small congregations is **intimate relationships**. Most in the small church know everyone else well; many are related by blood, and those who are not might as well be. The pastor knows everyone well, including recognizing out-of-town family members when they visit. In our hands-off culture where electronic communication has surpassed human interaction, where we barely know those who live next door to us, the small church offers a place where everybody knows your name and your story, and you can be yourself. Several of the small churches I know have a very personal, intimate prayer sharing time during worship. They are willing to ask for prayers for an addicted child or a divorcing friend because they know they are in a safe place with people who care about them.

Because of the intimacy of the relationships, **pastoral care** in the small church is often more personal than in larger churches. Parishioners receive a personal visit from the minister or priest when they are in the hospital. Many small-church pastors visit each person in the congregation from time to time. Communication is easier in the small church, so the word gets around when someone is in need. Congregation members take on a pastoral care function as well. They care about one another; they notice when one of the flock is missing for a couple of Sundays and check on them; they fill freezers and pantries when there is a death in the family. I have also noticed that in many cases the pastor is cared for by the congregation in a very personal way. The small church excels at caring for one another.

Lay involvement is often greater than in larger churches. You can't be anonymous in the small church, and visitors who stop by will know immediately they will have to be involved if they return to this church. As with any of these positive characteristics, there can also be a negative side. Because the workers are fewer, there is more work for each one to do. But because the workers are fewer, opportunities are greater to use one's gifts. The amateur artist can create works of art for the church which are loved and appreciated. Innovations from members are tried – a puppet ministry or an arts program – depending on the gifts of the members. If there is criticism, it is not because of the effort, it is because it wasn't shared earlier. Because the workers are fewer, the service of laypeople of all ages and circumstances is highly valued in the small church.

The **lack of bureaucracy** is cited by many small church pastors as a positive point. When something needs to get done, it can be done, rather than requiring permission and coordination with the other program staff and administrators – in the small church there aren't any! If a parishioner has an idea for a new ministry and can find another person who will help, the ministry will probably happen. Because of this lack of red tape, and probably also because of the intimacy of relationships, a congregation can be more creative. Something new can be tried in worship, and if it survives a second week, it becomes "the way we've always done it." Clergy who are less than excited about administration do well in the small church. They appreciate the flexibility of the schedule, and their availability to be involved in the community is greater.

It is important for leaders in the small church to recognize when the church is suffering from low self-esteem and work to correct it. It might be as simple as the language that is used when describing the church and its ministry: "We're just a small church." "We can't do that because we're too small." Change that to "Look what we can do because we're a small church." Be wary of measures of your congregation that focus on the negative – some congregational assessment programs identify the weaknesses in the congregation; look instead for models that primarily celebrate the strengths.

A Disciples of Christ church I visited in Indiana was down to 18 members, with 10-15 in church on an average Sunday. All were in their 70s or older, and they knew the church was going to close before too long. They began an "English as a Second Language" ministry in their church, providing some leadership (88 year-old Dorothy taught numbers) and snacks for the Hispanic participants (more about this in the Mission and Outreach chapter).

> **I enjoy small church ministry because worship doesn't begin until Jerome arrives. I enjoy small church ministry because, after I say "let us join together in the Lord's Prayer" there is a slight pause while everyone waits for Clell to say, "Our Father..." I enjoy small church ministry because our board meetings last about 15 minutes. I enjoy small church ministry because, after severe weather moves through our area, I can check on everyone by phone in an hour or so. I enjoy small church ministry because, when Nadia invited us to her first**

communion at St. Michael's Catholic church, we met early for our brief worship service and then we all (yes, all 18 of us that day) went to mass at St. Michael's for Nadia. I enjoy small church ministry because significant events that happen during the week (most often funerals, but sometimes a wedding or a birth) are talked about in worship when needed. I enjoy small church ministry because it's personal, everyone is noticed, one person can make a difference, one person is important. I enjoy small church ministry because life will not be ignored. Life in a small church demands attention and requires us to be present with each other as we participate in the mess and joy of living. I enjoy small church ministry because, good and bad – our life is lived out in the open. There is no place to hide in our pews or in our parking lot. We agree and disagree, we love and we fight right out in front of God and everybody.

Planning and Appreciative Inquiry

For congregations who are thinking about a visioning process, or are planning their ministries for the next couple of years, I recommend using Appreciative Inquiry (AI). AI began as a business model, moving companies off their "problem solving" model toward a more gifts-oriented model. For congregations, the best book I have seen on the topic is Mark Lau Branson's *Memories, Hopes, and Conversations: Appreciative Inquiry for Congregational Change*. Branson begins with Philippians 4:8: Finally, beloved, whatever is true, whatever is honorable, whatever is just, whatever is pure, whatever is commendable, if there is any excellence and if there is anything worthy of praise, think about these things (NRSV).

The ten assumptions of AI, according to Branson, are:

In every organizations, some things work well. AI assumes that even the most challenged and dispirited organization has stories and practices that can point toward a hopeful future. What works well here? What are we proud of? What draws us here?

What we focus on becomes our reality. The perceived reality of an organization is defined by whatever participants think about, talk about, work on, dream about, or plan. AI teaches that, while we do not need to dismiss the serious challenges we face or the lessons of previous mistakes, we need to center our attention on our strengths.

Asking questions influences the group. No research is truly neutral; the research itself changes a church by influencing the thinking and conversations and images of participants. Change begins with the very first questions.

People have more confidence in the journey to the future when they carry forward parts of the past. The unknown easily creates fears, and participants resist fear. Confidence and trust can be built when questions create direct links with the organization's best and most appreciated narratives.

If we carry parts of the past into the future, they should be what is best about the past. Generative change should displace meaningless structures and dysfunctional practices with the strengths of the organization's most life-giving narratives and behaviors.

It is important to value differences. When an organization tells its stories and works together to interpret them, everyone gains if mutual respect and attentiveness is the norm.

The language we use creates our reality. The words we use influences, positively or negatively, the reality of the group.

Organizations are heliotropic. This botanical term refers to plants' tendency to lean towards the sun. Similarly, organizations lean toward the source of energy, whether it is healthy or not.

Outcomes should be useful. Following conversations, the data is brought to an interpretive process in order to help participants envision and create their way towards a hopeful and fruitful future. While there may be emotional benefits from "just talking," AI assumes we are doing more – we are constructing.

All steps are collaborative. AI is not a process of giving stories and ideas to experts who then create a plan for everyone. Every phase requires wide participation – interviews, interpretation, visioning, embedding changes.[15]

The goal of AI in churches is to identify the things in the past, present, and future that bring life and energy and passion to the congregation. This is unlike some other visioning models where lists of congregational strengths and weaknesses are identified, and then the church puts its energy into their weakest areas. In the AI model, the strongest areas in the life of the church are identified and built upon. The way it works (and this is a very bare-bones explanation; buy the book for all the details) is that people in the church engage in one-on-one conversations with other church members, and explore together the following three questions:

- Remembering your entire experience at our church, when were you most alive, most motivated and excited about your involvement? What made it exciting? Who else was involved? What happened? What was your part? Describe what you felt.

- What do you value most about our church? What activities or ingredients or ways of life are most important?

- Make three wishes for the future of this church.[16]

Everyone in the congregation who wants to participate in the process can. This is not only the board members engaging in looking at the future of the church, but everyone. While this may seem inconsistent with your congregation's theology and polity, the fact is that leaders aren't leaders if they don't have any followers; the entire congregation should have input into its future direction. Where the board comes in is after the conversations are completed. The board then identifies common themes in the responses, and works to prioritize and develop those themes.

I like to introduce the AI process to the church board and any others interested – perhaps the deacons or the planning committee, if there is one. We run through the assumptions and then try out the questions in pairs. Then, over the next few weeks, those leaders engage in conversations with others in the church. The questions are fun and non-threatening, and most people (though not all!) are comfortable with them.

AI is not about writing a mission statement; it is about identifying values and priorities and strengths and engaging in them in as excellent a way as possible. After the board identifies the common themes, I would add two more questions for their consideration:

- What is going on in the local community you serve? Think particularly of those persons who are not a part of your congregation. What are the strongest realities? What needs exist? Where are people hurting? Where are there opportunities to be in ministry with the community?

- If you could choose one issue for this congregation to focus its energy on in the year ahead, what would it be?

This moves the ministry outside the walls of the church, which is a growing edge for many small congregations, and into the local community, and it keeps things manageable. The worst thing a small congregation can do is identify 12 goals for the coming year and expect those few leaders in the church to make them happen. Everything needs to be done slowly, in small steps.

The reasons I think Appreciative Inquiry is a good process for small congregations is that it fits; it is based on those things that small congregations do well:

- It is relational in nature. This is not a survey one fills out, it is a conversation. Most people are willing to open up a little to one other person, although they might not speak up in front of the whole church. I have encountered a couple of people over the years who balk at these AI conversations, but not too many. If you are in the small church, it is likely you can be comfortable with talking to another person.

- It is collaborative. Everyone who wants a voice is offered the opportunity to participate. This is consensus-seeking at its best. Throughout the process, let the congregation know they were heard, and even if their idea for the future is not the one chosen for this year, it might be for next.

- It empowers laypeople. I usually suggest the pastor not participate in the conversation groups, since responses might not be quite as honest or forthright if the other person is the pastor. AI is not about bringing in a consultant to tell you what to do, it is about the congregation generating its own responses, making its own choices, and taking responsibility for its own future.

- It honors the past, but doesn't dwell in it. Small congregations are deeply rooted in tradition, and the AI process sees the value in that. The first question is about the stories of the past. AI seeks to bring forward what was good from the congregation's history, and leave the mistakes where they belong: in the past.

- It is about conversation and story. When I visit a small congregation, I only have to say, "Tell me about your church," and I can expect 45 minutes of stories. We are a people rooted in our stories. AI encourages participants to tell their own personal stories.

- It emphasizes the positive. So many small congregations have issues with low self-esteem. From the foundational scripture to the final visioning process, it looks for the best and doesn't try to push people into doing things about which they have no energy.

- There is no cost to participate in AI! No workbooks, no consultant, no fees. The most you need to spend is the cost of the book (and when you purchase it the publisher, The Alban Institute, allows you access to all of the outlines and questions online to download).

Clergy and the Small Church

Clergy are usually not trained to minister in the small church while they are in seminary,[17] and they graduate assuming they will serve a church like the one from which they came – often a program or corporate church. Some begin to look for a position, and somewhat reluctantly take a call in a small church so they can "do their time," with the full intention that after a couple of years they will then be able to seek and find a call to a larger church. The small church becomes the stepping stone to a "real" church. I know a Lutheran pastor who chose to take a call with a small congregation, and had to defend his choice to his colleagues. They assumed he had done something to make the bishop mad, and being placed in a small church was his punishment.

It becomes a cycle, a self-fulfilling prophecy of sorts. Small congregations don't attract quality clergy (often because of low salaries or remote locations, or both), or if they do, the pastor stays for only a short time and then leaves for greener grass.

I've even seen congregations get very nervous when you tell them they are blessed with an excellent pastor, because they assume that if their pastor is excellent, he or she will be snatched up by a better offer (bigger, more prestigious, more money, etc.). In that case some congregations, to steel themselves for what they think is inevitable hurt and loss, begin to act out toward the pastor. One Lutheran congregation I visited in Vermont had enjoyed a healthy seven-year pastorate, but then the pastor reported that the congregation seemed to turn on her for no apparent reason. They were being difficult at Council meetings, picking fights, disagreeing when they had not done so before. She was baffled until she looked at the congregation's history and discovered that most of their former pastors had left at the seven- or eight-year mark. She went out of her way to reassure people that she was staying, and by the time she made it through the eighth year, things were back to normal. In order to protect themselves from the (perceived) inevitable loss of the pastor, they subconsciously decided they would "leave" her first by looking for ways to break the ties and emotional bonds they had with her.

Young and/or newly ordained clergy can be a blessing to a small church, provided they stay for a reasonable length of time. They can bring new ideas, new life, and new hope to a congregation that might be stale and inwardly focused. They might bring young children into a congregation full of surrogate grandparents. Properly trained young clergy will know enough to do a lot of observing of the systems of the congregation before jumping in to make changes. It takes at least five years for a pastor to develop the trust that is necessary to lead a change process. Jason Byassee, in his book, *The Gifts of the Small Church*, recounts his two-year adventure with a small United Methodist congregation in North Carolina with humor and well-told stories interspersed with important theological observations. My only criticism of his work is that he only stayed two years!

The other segment of the clergy population over-represented in the small church are those who are retired or are close to retirement. There is often less pressure and usually less bureaucracy in the small church, and this is a lower-stress way to end one's professional career. Retired clergy are often attractive to small congregations because there is a cap on the amount of money they can make and still retain their retired status, so they can work for less than a pastor with a family or children in college. Older clergy also connect well with congregations made up of mostly older members, as many small churches are. They bring a wisdom that connects with congregants, a wealth of experience to share, and a deep and authentic faith. The concerns with older and retired clergy are that they may not be transformational in their approach, so they may be very good at maintenance in a small church – keeping all the trains running on time - but not so good at mission – bringing new ideas that will bring new life to the congregation.

Pastors, denominations, and search committees should pay attention to the diversity of gifts we are given by God for ministry. Regardless of the pressures of the culture to move up the ladder, some clergy are just not gifted for larger church ministry. I know a pastor who was on the typical track – he successfully served a small congregation, and then moved to a newly chartered church that was growing rapidly. He was not particularly gifted in administration, and as the church grew, he got more and more buried in bureaucracy. His gifts were in preaching and pastoral care. But when the pressure got to be too much at the growing church, he moved to an even larger church. It was no surprise that he wasn't happy there. After a very stressful couple of years, he left pastoral ministry altogether, and went to work for a church-related business. Many years later, he still works for the business, but is also the supply preacher/pastor for a very small church on the weekends. He loves the congregation and they love him. Clearly, this pastor was gifted for small church ministry and had to go through a lot of pain, even leaving the pastoral ministry, before he recognized it.

If we accept the premise that there is value in the small congregation, then we must look at ways to make small churches the best witnesses to God's Kingdom that they can be. For the next five chapters, we're going to look at five important areas of small church life and health – worship and preaching, Christian education, congregational and self care, mission and outreach, and leadership. Obviously, all of these are important areas of ministry, and none can be ignored. Some churches, however, will put extra emphasis on some over others due to circumstances (there's no sense in having a children's ministry if all of the parishioners are over the age of sixty), but each one should be carefully thought through in trying to best fulfill the Great Commandment – "You shall love the Lord your God with all with all your heart, and with all your soul, and with all your mind . . . You shall love your neighbor as yourself" (Matthew 22:37, 39). That, by the way, is a pretty good place to start when working on a mission statement.

These chapters will give examples from small churches that were part of the Summer Collegium, or small churches I know in other contexts. They are not meant to be prescriptions to follow exactly; they are meant to inspire your congregation toward excellence and best practices of its own. Remember, your context will be different from those whose stories you will hear in these pages.

3

PROCLAIMING THE GOOD NEWS
WORSHIP AND PREACHING

The first and probably foremost experience the congregation and visitors will experience is worship. We generally connect the notion of "church" with Sunday morning, and with the worship experience. It makes sense that worship can have a great impact on the life and health of the congregation. What is the goal of worship? For one congregation it may be to bring people together for a family reunion each Sunday. Or, it may be the only time for members and friends to hear teaching from the Bible. Sadly, for some, worship is primarily a time to take up the collection. Think about the last time you had to cancel church because of bad weather: was your biggest worry whether you could make up the offering that would be missed? Sometimes we lose our focus when we are so concerned about keeping the church alive, and we forget why we are a church and why we come to worship.

The goal of worship ought to be to bring people closer to God and allow them to offer prayer and thanksgiving in the company of other Christians. This may seem obvious, but we don't always practice this way. The most important focus in worship is God, not ourselves. We run the risk of becoming self-centered when we come to worship to get something; this is the time we come to give something to God. Pastors and lay people alike worry about the worship experience – will I be able to pronounce those names properly when I read the scripture? Will my sermon be funny or interesting enough? Am I wearing the right clothes? Are those teenagers going to come in jeans again? What will *I* get out of worship this week? When we worry about these things, our focus is on ourselves and not on God. The worship experience should draw us into God's presence with awe and respect, with wonder and a keen sense of mystery.

If We Just Got a Rock Band, We'd Attract Young People

Once in awhile I turn on one of the evangelical mega-church programs as I'm getting ready for church on Sunday morning. As someone who loves the small church, it's hard to find many things I have in common with that type of worship, but it is pretty impressive to see the large numbers of people gathered. Members of small churches look at these congregations and wonder how they attract so many people, when their congregation struggles to get 30 on an average Sunday. For many of these folks, the mega-churches are not just TV churches; they are in the towns in which their churches have been located for two hundred years. The new church comes in and builds a structure with a gymnasium and stadium seating and a loud praise band for worship, and a charismatic preacher and youth director, and suddenly all of the young people in town want to go there. The small congregation loses the few teenagers it has and wonders, "What can we do to get young people to come back to our churches for worship?" or worse, "If we could afford a gym or fancy sound equipment or just had a younger minister, we could be a large church, too." So, in a last-ditch effort to bring new life to their congregation, they sink their last dollars into expensive equipment or an expensive staff person. Often, what they end up with is not exactly what they had hoped for: they have spent all of ther money and the only thing they have to show for it is a lot of "stuff" and an existing congregation that doesn't find this type of worship worshipful, and is considering attending the other small church down the road.

There is no panacea for turning worship attendance around, and churches who try to be something they are not will pay the price in failing to meet the needs of those who are already there. The goal of worship is to bring people closer to God, and if no one is there to experience worship, that probably won't happen.

Remember our list of characteristics of healthy small churches. How can some of those be built up to make worship in the small church meaningful to parishioners and pleasing to God?

- Intimate relationships – Pastoral prayers can be intimate expressions of loving and caring in the small church. People genuinely care for one another and are willing to be vulnerable in sharing their joys and concerns.

- People in the small church adapt to change for the sake of relationships – Innovative ideas can be tried in the small church without a lot of red tape, and folks will generally be willing to try something on a trial basis, provided it is introduced slowly by a pastor who has earned their trust, or by a trusted church leader.

- Storytelling – We Christians are a story people. The worship experience itself can be a creative re-telling of the stories of Scripture and other stories of our faith easily in the context of the small church.

- Intergenerational – The small church is happiest when the family is all together. Planning worship with people of all ages and circumstances involved together can be more meaningful to everyone present.

- Using everyone's gifts and talents – Small congregations are ideal places for people to test out their gifts and talents in a safe, accepting environment. Nine-year old Bobby's trumpet solo in "God of Our Fathers"[18] might have included some squeaks and stops, but everyone in church was lifted up by hearing it and never heard those mistakes, because Bobby is one of their own and they love him. Would Bobby have been given a chance to play his trumpet in the big church with the excellent music program for which they are known?

Some small congregations have faced real angst over someone, usually the pastor, wanting to put in large screens at the front of the sanctuary, either to display announcements, artistic images, the liturgy, the music, or any combination of these. Screens can be effective in taking worship out of being such a verbal-linguistic event and involving others of our intelligences, such as artistic and visual. If your congregation wants to try using a screen in worship, make sure you think carefully about why you want it. If the best reason you can come up with is that the big successful church on the outskirts of town uses one, that's not good enough.

A number of years ago, I did an exercise with some children in the church. I gave them the hymn, "God of the Sparrow"[19] which is full of visual imagery, and asked them to illustrate it on large paper, one phrase per page. The idea was that the congregation could sing it using the visual clues while looking up, and not sing it into their hymnal. I am always amused when "Jesus Loves Me" is one of the hymn selections and people still have to have those hymnals open and turned to the right page so they can read the words! It occurs to me now that having words and images up front in worship as a way to get people to look up as they sang God's praises was a precursor to having screens to do the very same thing.

The problem I have with screens for hymns is that most churches project only the words on the screen. I am not an auditory learner, and many others have the same problem I do: if the tune is not familiar, I have nowhere to look to figure it out. I usually just stand there silently, even though I love to sing hymns! This is especially the case when the musician (or the CD player) doesn't run through the hymn once before we are asked to start singing. Imagine my delight when I visited a small Christian Reformed Church outside of Detroit and they had words and music projected on their screen!

Screens aren't inherently bad, but can be badly used. And having parts of worship projected on a screen is not the answer to a church's decline.

Looking for a one-size-fits-all approach to increasing worship attendance will not work in the small church. Copying what works in the mega-church often results in alienating the people who like the intimacy and hominess of the small congregation. A better approach will be to discover the uniqueness of your particular church's identity and build on that.

Authentic and Relevant Worship

Worship is for glorifying and praising God, and for helping people to learn more about this God whom we worship and praise, so that our faithfulness might be increased. It is not a show or a performance. Here's the definition of worship in the Presbyterian Church (U.S.A.) constitution:

> Christian worship joyfully ascribes all praise and honor, glory and power to the triune God. In worship the people of God acknowledge God present in the world and in their lives. As they respond to God's claim and redemptive action in Jesus Christ, believers are transformed and renewed. In worship the faithful offer themselves to God and are equipped for God's service in the world.[20]

Your denomination's definition of worship is probably not much different. It is well to have this kind of worship statement in mind as you look at how to shape the worship in any congregation so that it best transforms and renews those who participate.

Two words to keep in mind to help a congregation to be all that it can be and to have the best shot at attracting new members into your family of faith and bringing them closer to God, are authentic and relevant. Authenticity means being real about who you are, what the gifts and talents of your members are, what your dreams and visions are for the future, what your mission is, and how it all fits into God's story. Not the hopes and dreams of the other churches in town, but yours. As mentioned earlier, using a process such as Appreciative Inquiry to get at those things can be helpful, especially because it is focused on your church and not what a consultant or the latest fad in church growth literature tells you to do and be. The people of the congregation will not have the energy for ministry that you want and need if it is not uniquely them. This is not to say that they cannot be stretched and cannot grow; in the comfort of the familiar they will be able to look at their situation and be willing to take some risks.

Relevant worship and ministry goes hand-in-hand with the authentic. Not only does your ministry need to be real, and be a reflection of the congregation, but people who are searching for faith are also searching for relevance. This should be reflected in sermons that not only explain the biblical texts and their original meaning, but also include examples that relate to the people in the congregation – all of the people, including children, youth, young adults, middle adults and older adults. It's not only about what the Bible says, but about how I can live that out in my own life, and how my faithful understanding of that scripture will make a difference in the world. I hear it from young people all the time: what does that stuffy church with the dress codes and the old music and the boring sermons have to do with me? That's not just a self-centered attitude, but it is one for a generation that has many pulls on its time and its resources. Why should they choose church? In discerning your congregation's mission, and especially its worship, think about these things.

Beware of looking for that one thing that will turn your church around; be even more wary if it is something that large churches are doing, or something that costs a lot of money. There are probably other factors at play in those "successes." Instead, be on the lookout for what God wants you to do, what will bless God and further God's work on earth, and what will move the congregation to greater faithfulness.

Innovative Worship

It is a joy in the small church to be able to try some new things without an act of Congress to do it. A pastor with some creativity can go a long way in making worship unique and meaningful to those present. It may sound as if I am refuting what I said earlier about tradition and the small church, but sometimes larger churches are even more bound by their traditions when "we've always done it that way" becomes the reason to hold back on new ideas. Perhaps some smaller churches realize that "the way we've always done things" isn't working, and they need to try new things. Maybe they allow the pastor some latitude because they love him and are willing to cut him some slack!

It is even better if a group of interested people from the church can be assembled to plan the Advent season worship services or the mid-week Lenten program, or a summer worship series. I saw this work well in the Washington, D.C. church I joined while living near there.

> **A group of about 10 people gathered several months before Advent and brainstormed ideas for the season, using the Lectionary scriptures. The pastor contributed to the discussion, but did not dominate it. Ideas began flowing about a mission emphasis that**

could work alongside the worship, and how that could be brought into the worship, hymns that could be used each week, and a Bible study that could run during the season. It was a great collaboration, and worked well in that congregation of bright, creative people. The following Lent, they planned the season around visual images and drama, and each Sunday in Lent a group of three or four from the church enacted a drama in place of the sermon, which portrayed a modern interpretation of the Bible story for the week. This church welcomes about 75 on an average Sunday.

A United Church of Christ congregation in Eastern Oregon has a "Bring an Object" Sunday once a quarter. The pastor does not prepare a sermon for that day, but invites people in the congregation to bring any interesting object to church. Objects are put in a basket as folks walked in, and the pastor collects them as he entered the service. On the Sunday I was there for the sermon, he pulled things out of the basket and told a Bible story related to the object. There were four or five different objects he used, and told four or five different stories, from the anointing of Jesus with expensive perfume (the object was an intricate jar someone had found on a vacation to Europe), to the healing of the blind man (the object was a pair of glasses). This was one way this congregation engaged its members in the Bible as part of the worship – people enjoyed it because they did not know where the pastor would go with the object, and it became a kind of "stump the pastor" event. (I don't think he was stumped very often!)

Not too far away, in an Episcopal Church in Idaho, the first service evolved into an interesting pattern (many small Episcopal churches have two services, often an early service with a very short liturgy and no music, and a later, more traditional service). In this particular church, at the early service, the congregation of about 20 was gathered into a circle and the liturgy proceeded. When it came time for the sermon, the scriptures of the day were read and discussed by everyone. The priest had his sermon prepared on the texts for the later service, so he merely guided the group with questions to get to his sermon points.

An Anglican Church in Nova Scotia has a long history of lay preaching; this has been encouraged by successive clergy, and lay people preach every fifth Sunday.

From the pastor of a 13-year-old Presbyterian Church in Georgia: "Our worship can best be described as blended, relatively informal, with a variety of music and styles. The most unique aspect of our worship is that no one says: 'But we've always done it this way.' In serving nearly three years, we have had drama, puppet shows, youth-led worship, children helping with the Lord's Supper, last minute changes and more, and the universal response is, 'Let's do it!' We are a relatively young church – half under 50 years old. And as a new congregation, even our senior members have an open, engaging attitude."

None of these ideas is earth-shattering or profound, but they do illustrate that creative ministry can be and is being done in small churches across the country. The important thing is to look at the context in which the congregation is planted, and the gifts and skills of the people who are part of the congregation, and try some new things. They will tell you if they hate it. As mentioned earlier, often when something new is tried in a small church, it needs only happen two or three times and it becomes part of the culture – the "we've always done it that way."

Music and Music Styles

"Music is the nuclear reactor of congregational worship," says Tom Long. "It is where much of the radioactive material is stored, where a good bit of the energy is generated, and, alas, where congregational meltdown is most likely to occur. Change the order of worship, and you may set off a debate. Change the music, and you may split the congregation."[21] This is true in large churches and in small. Music touches our souls, moves us emotionally in ways that words cannot. Regardless of your age, upbringing, training, or preference, most people are affected by the music and music choices that are made in the church. I am not about to say that young people always like praise choruses or rock music, any more than I will say that older folks only like the classics. It all depends on your own preference. Churches make mistakes in thinking that a certain kind of music will necessarily attract a certain type of worshiper. But if a church's music does not move a worshiper in some way, it may be a reason for them not to return. Because of the importance of music in worship (or, in some churches, not having music in worship), it can become an emotional and highly charged topic of discussion if changes are to be made.

In small churches, the challenge is often finding musicians who are dependable and talented, and yet are affordable. Many small congregations use volunteers from the congregation, often retired music teachers or amateur musicians. Fortunate is the church that is situated near a college or university and can secure the services of music students or professors. Sometimes small churches cannot afford to pay, and are grateful for anyone who can lead the congregation in their hymns.

Some small congregations use a blending of different styles of church music to attract and keep people with various preferences. This can be great if it's done carefully and well. Some congregations have one particular style of music, and that reflects their personality; it is who they are. The reasons for choosing a particular type of music should be thought through carefully with the musician, if there is one, along with others who are interested, and the pastor should always be included in that discussion.

What about a small church that has no musician? There are a couple of options. One is that you can buy CD music from your denomination that will accompany the hymns in your hymnal. Many of these are pretty good and can certainly help when that's your only option. The trouble is that the tempo of the music is up to the CD, and not the congregation.

Another option is to sing a cappella. We were fortunate in the Summer Collegium to have the Rev. Dr. John Bell, from the Iona Community in Scotland, as our musician two of the years. John has written numerous songs for unaccompanied congregational singing. He simply practices the music with the congregation before worship, lining it out with his hands and dividing the congregation into parts. The songs are simple and are repeated several times, but it's amazing how good the sound is! Iona music is available on CD and in music books.[22] Many small congregations have found Taizé music and music from Iona to be easy to sing a cappella and very worshipful.

If significant changes are to be made in the music of the congregation, make sure they are done slowly and intentionally, with major buy-in from the congregation. Sometimes the fear of change can be worse than the actual change, so try new things out before completely changing everything. If you want to add praise choruses to your repertoire, add 15 or 30 minutes on the beginning of your service for praise music. Even trying unfamiliar hymns from your hymnal can be a challenge. But try out some new music once in awhile anyway. Use rhythm instruments in trying out that snappy Spanish hymn. Play a new hymn as a prelude before introducing it. One church I know uses a new hymn every Sunday for a month as a way of introducing it into the congregation's repertoire.

One note about praise choruses: take care that you are not sending a message you don't want to send. Look at the theology present in the song, and be sure it matches your denomination's tradition. Many praise choruses are focused on an individual (not Jesus!); you'll find a lot of "I" and "me" language. The subject of the song becomes the singer, and not the one being sung to and about. In the PCUSA we have a supplemental hymnal that includes some praise music (as well as Taizé and songs from the Iona community), and I am comfortable that the music in there is in line with Reformed Theology.

> **From the pastor of a United Methodist Church in Wisconsin – "[Our church] is distinctive for its music ministry which is led by a longtime volunteer music director. She conducts a four-octave hand bell choir, the vocal choir, and she nurtures many young musicians in the congregation. For the past three years a Holy Week drama, 'The Living Last Supper,' has been presented in our congregation and to congregations in neighboring communities. Thirteen men and youth from the church play the roles of Jesus' disciples, with the choir providing choral music to accompany the drama."**

One small United Methodist congregation in rural Minnesota was part of a two-point charge. The pastor warned me before we went to the second congregation that morning. Their pianist was a much-loved woman in her 90s who had grown up playing honky-tonk music, and when she played the traditional hymns, they all had an undertone of that style of music!

From a Lutheran Church in North Carolina: "[This congregation] is a rather new congregation that was established six years ago. Two small congregations dissolved their ministries to come together as a congregation. We are currently worshipping in the 45 year-old building that once housed one of the congregations. The predecessor congregations were very different in terms of their preferred worship style – one traditional, one contemporary. Currently we worship using a blended style of worship. Our traditional liturgy incorporates both traditional and contemporary styles of music."

Making Changes in Worship – Proceed with Caution!

I know that when it comes to worship in small congregations, we often see a lot of fussing over seemingly unimportant things. I always caution seminary students and new pastors in small congregations to be very careful about making any changes in worship until they've been there for a while. We've all heard the stories of new pastors who come into the church in their first call and decide to move the baptismal font two feet to the left, causing a major conflict in the church, and even putting their jobs in jeopardy! A church I was part of had a pastor who was there for nearly 30 years, and just before he left, someone said, "Now that [the pastor] is leaving, I think we ought to include the words to the Apostles' Creed and the Doxology and the Gloria Patri in the bulletin." It's not a bad idea, but you can bet some people in the congregation had big problems with that. It's better to make those changes slowly and deliberately. It seems silly, though, doesn't it. "We've always done it that way" keeps us from putting our attention on what is really important: the worship and praise of God. Changing the elements of worship, or the liturgy, or the furniture can be difficult for those who find comfort in the familiar, though, and should be handled with great care and intentionality.

Because the small church is so relational, change must be undertaken with an appreciation for the importance of relationships. Traditions must be known and respected. Bush and O'Reilly suggest that one should:

- Make changes on a trial basis, which gives everyone the opportunity to experience the change for awhile and evaluate it, but doesn't force people to commit to something completely.

- Explain the changes clearly, and make clear the avenues to express observations and impressions; leaders must allow for variations on their vision and to hear and respect the improvements.

- Congregations can be remarkably forgiving of leaders who are prepared to admit missteps. However, don't rely too much on the "forgiveness is easier to get than permission" mantra – you have to have a lot of capital in your 'trust bank' for that to occur.[23]

Take a look at the space for worship. Does it support the personality and makeup of the congregation? If a small congregation meets in worship space designed for hundreds of people, a visitor may be intimidated by that, especially because a large space makes a small congregation look even smaller. I have learned that not only do Presbyterians prefer to fill the back rows first, so do parishioners of all denominations. If the sanctuary is massive, the congregation will be divided and the intimacy small churches are so good at will be compromised. Look for ways to make the room seem smaller, by moving the lofty pulpit closer to the people or roping off several rows in the back so the "back row" is closer to the front. One congregation I know remodeled their sanctuary so that the seating space was smaller and the narthex area was much larger, making it appropriate for coffee hour following worship. Look at the worship space with the theology of your tradition in mind – if your tradition sees clergy and lay people on a relatively even plain, then preaching from a pulpit that is far from the congregation and is in a place "on-high" doesn't support that theology.

It never hurts when making changes, even small ones, to have backup. Get a group – perhaps the worship committee if there is one –but definitely including the church musician and perhaps some of the more opinionated members, and discuss ideas you have for changes. If they can see your reasoning, they will be more likely to support you to others who might complain. Make changes slowly, with lots of preparation, and your chances of success will increase dramatically.

Accessible Worship

While there are exciting, innovative elements to worship that are unique to small churches, we must not become so small-minded that we forget that we might have visitors in our midst. Take a look at your worship experience from the point of view of an outsider; or better yet, invite a friend or neighbor to come to worship and ask them some questions later. Much of this can fall under the category of outreach, but it is also relevant here. Here are examples of things to look for as you view your worship from the perspective of a visitor, along with the implications:

- Could you find a parking space close to the building? (Are members keeping all of the prime spots?)

- Could you tell which door to enter for worship? (Are there signs pointing to the sanctuary?)

- Was someone there to greet you at the door? (or were they absent, or worse, chatting with one another and not paying any attention?)

- Were you handed a bulletin? (or does the "in crowd" know how the service goes without one?)

- Were you escorted to a seat and introduced to someone sitting nearby? (It's no fun to walk into a new church and not be able to connect with anyone.)

- Was the bulletin clear as to when to stand and when to sit; what book/s to use when; when the leader speaks and when the people speak; where to find the Lord's Prayer, Doxology, Gloria Patri, or other elements most members know by heart; if particular musical pieces are used after the offering or the benediction, are words and music printed or referenced? (Are only insiders able to follow the order of worship and participate fully?)

- If you are celebrating the Lord's Supper that day, is it clear a) who may partake of the meal? b) whether the bread and cup are passed or done by intinction or served at the front? c) if you pass the elements, is the bread to be held until all can partake together or eaten when it is received? d) if you serve the elements at the front, is there a standard response upon receiving the Sacrament? (Is this an exclusive dinner party, or is it communion with one another?)

- If you got lost in any part of the service, did someone sitting near you offer to help? (Or were you left to figure it out or not participate?)

- Were bulletin announcements clear for a visitor? (My favorite bulletin announcement is: "If you'd like to join the ladies' group, come to Mary's house on Tuesday or give her a call." Just who is Mary, where does she live, and what is her phone number?)

- Were you greeted by several members during the passing of the peace? Small churches often have what one medium sized church member called "an excruciatingly long passing of the peace." This is because every Sunday is like a family reunion in the small church, and everyone greets everyone else. (Are visitors included in God's family that day?)

- Did anyone talk to you at the coffee hour? (Many small churches are good at the greeting during the service, but then get in their groups to do business or catch up on news, leaving visitors with no one to talk to.)

I think you get the point. It might be surprising how many "insider" elements there are in one congregation's worship service. Look for them and correct them. Take a look at the YouTube video about visitors at worship, if you haven't seen it. It is a good way to broach the subject with your leaders.[24]

Another thing we joke about, but is unfortunaely too often true, is the fact that in small churches it is likely that a regular member "owns" his or her pew. Everyone in the congregation knows which pews they sit in, and they seldom change. If a visitor shows up and sits in "your" pew, what do you do? I know of a church in which a long-time member arrived to find visitors in her pew and asked them to move. They did – right out the door!

Worship is the experience upon which visitors will make their decisions about returning or not. A particular congregation has only one chance to show the visitor who they really are.   What impression will you give?

Following are some more statements on worship experiences in the small church:

>**From a Presbyterian Church member in Florida:** "We've been a very small congregation but now we're growing. We've hung on when others thought the church didn't have a chance to survive; now we're thriving. We love one another and try to find varieties of ways to love others. We laugh about our 'Moment to Meet' in worship because it goes on so long and everybody is up and greeting everybody else, so it's sometimes hard to re-gather us. We blend lots of styles in our worship because we use a choir and a praise band, an organ and a piano. Sometimes we use drama as the sermon. Using a screen and PowerPoint has allowed some of our older members to sing again (since the hymnal print was too small) and also provides a ministry for our teenagers who love to run the slides (it keeps them alert). What most people note is that our worship is not stuffy so visitors feel at ease when they come. It's never boring! Our monthly healing service touches those who attend in a way weekly worship can't – silence is sometimes hard to find in our frantic lives. It brings in people who worship in other congregations as well.

>**From the pastor of a United Church of Christ church in Seattle:** "We call ourselves 'small but mighty.' The building is used by over 50 twelve-step groups welcoming up to 1500 people each week. About half of our membership claims a twelve-step story, which in turns makes our worship and prayer life particularly faithful, vital, and honest." The sharing of prayers of the people in this church is unlike most others: people allow themselves to be vulnerable; the Sunday I visited there were prayers for a child who was falling back into addiction, and prayers from another person who found herself struggling with alcoholism. There was never a hint that they would be negatively judged. This was clearly a safe place.

Worship is perhaps the most visible event for visitors to and members of the small congregation. Make sure the worship experience is meaningful – perhaps more easily done in a congregation where everyone knows everyone – and relevant. The purpose of worship should bring people closer to God and one another in every aspect and activity. This may seem obvious, but when we get wrapped up in the details that have nothing to do with praising and honoring God, it can deaden an experience that should be filled with joy, awe, and mystery. It's a question of leadership and discipleship. "Meaningful worship happens in congregations of all sizes. All congregations hold services where people feel joy and inspiration. These congregational strengths do not depend on size. But what predicts beyond-the-ordinary performance [in] meaningful worship? Two factors matter: congregations that have empowering leaders and worshipers who are growing spiritually."[25]

4

TELLING THE STORY

CHRISTIAN EDUCATION

While there is not a lot of question that worship is a necessary component for "being church," Christian education is often not seen as so necessary. There is an assumption in some congregations and denominations that Christian education means educating children, and if a small church has no children, the congregation has no need to worry about Christian education. Nothing could be further from the truth. We live in a country where biblical illiteracy is rampant. Many of the adults who come to church are those people who left the church after their confirmation, so they are equipped with an 8th or 9th grade Christian education. More and more people in the pews have no background in the stories of the faith, so references made in a sermon about David and Goliath or Abraham and Sarah are lost on them. It is imperative that adults as well as children take the task of faith formation seriously.

The first piece of advice I offer to those who are considering starting or pumping up the program of educational ministries in their small congregations is to take it back to basics – ask yourself and your leaders what they see as the goal of education in the church. Just as worship is a way to further the faith development of God's people, so education will do the same, giving people a language and a history and a connection with the faithful throughout history. That connection with the saints brings people closer to God and to a faith that has depth.

They Gave Us Permission to Think Outside the Box!

That was what an excited Lutheran pastor told her congregation after experiencing a workshop on Christian Education at the Summer Collegium. Her congregation had been struggling with not having enough children for a "critical mass," whatever that is, on Sunday morning for Sunday school. Teachers would prepare lessons, and week after week there would be one or two or no children there to teach. It was frustrating for the teachers and frustrating for the pastor. But they were pulled by the notion that a church should have Sunday school classes for children.

Many congregations get hung up on the practical aspects of Christian education. "We don't have enough (fill in the blank) teachers, children, classes, money for curriculum." Perhaps the most frustrating is, "Visitors who come with children look around and see that we don't have any, then don't return. If just two families with children would stay, then we'd have children and could attract more children!"

While larger congregations spend a lot of money on curriculum resources, small churches usually don't have much money to spend, especially on children's programming when children are only occasionally there. Generally speaking, folks in the small church do not rely so much on the curricular materials from the denomination; they are more interested in relational types of education – telling stories of the faith, sharing stories of people who have been influential in their personal faith walk, remembering the ancestors of faith in their particular church. Small congregations are people of story. From the beginning of time, faithful people everywhere have also been people of story. Our faith was handed down for generations using storytelling, repeating the stories of faithful women and men to keep the faith tradition fresh and relevant. "Keep these words that I am commanding you today in your heart. Recite them to your children and talk about them when you are at home and when you are away, when you lie down and when you rise. Bind them as a sign on your hand, fix them as an emblem on your forehead, and write them on the doorposts of your house and on your gates"

(Deuteronomy 6:6-9). This type of sharing can bring the scriptures to life, and also make it easier for new people to become part of the story. It requires a little "out of the box" thinking.

Christian formation should be something in the DNA of the congregation, and not dependent on how many children there are or about dividing people into age groupings. Get back to the basics. What is the overarching goal of Christian education/formation in the church, in any church? Don Griggs and Judy Walther say it this way: "In small and large churches, in city and rural churches, in well-established and new churches, in churches everywhere, the challenge is the same – to present the gospel of Jesus Christ in ways that are compelling and memorable so that persons of all ages and circumstances will be nurtured in the Christian faith in order to be empowered to live faithfully as disciples of Jesus Christ."[26]

Once you have a good primary statement about Christian education, begin to focus in on your congregation. What do you want your efforts in Christian education and faith formation to accomplish in your particular congregation? Some responses (for better or worse) might be:

- To teach Bible stories.
- To teach children how to worship.
- To teach the traditions of your denomination.
- To teach about a Christian response to particular topics and issues in the world.
- To have time to make new friends and build relationships in the context of church.
- To memorize Scripture.
- To have a place for children to go while adults worship.
- Because a real church has Sunday School: "we've always done it that way".
- Because we have to compete with the other churches in town.

Look at some of the uniqueness and values of small congregations: the intimacy of relationships, the ability to be flexible and creative in programming, the idea that every individual is valued and important, the accessibility of the pastor, are some things that come to mind. How do these lists compare? What are the challenging points in connecting the two? What are some ways you might look differently at educational ministry because the congregation is small?

Narrow the lists down to what is really important. If you find yourself saying, "That is important because that's the way they did it when I was a kid, or in the larger church we came from," remember that your congregation is unique and cries out for unique solutions. Build on your strengths; build on your strengths! Perhaps intergenerational education will work best in your situation. Maybe the best education can be done in the context of the worship service. Maybe combining forces with other small churches in town will accomplish your goals. Or perhaps some people in your congregation have particular gifts that can be used to enhance your educational ministry – you may have people with skills in drama or music that could present the stories in new and engaging ways.

The important thing is to start with the basics – those purposes and goals for education that are the same for all Christians – then move into the specifics, checking back with the basics to make sure your particular circumstances don't outweigh the bigger picture.

The Lutheran pastor who was so excited about thinking outside the box talked to her Council about changing the expectations for children on Sunday morning. Instead of Sunday school, they started a mid-week program that met twice a month and fit better into sports schedules and energy levels. Those mid-week events include all ages, with a community meal and Bible studies and music and sharing. All it took was permission to think outside the box!

Children's Ministry

In many small congregations I have visited, folks are anxious to hear about ways to bring more children and youth into the church so they can feel like a "real" church, by having a Sunday school program. Christian education in the small church may not look the same as the faith formation programs in larger churches, but it should nonetheless be an important part of the ministry of the congregation.

The Schedule Let me say at the outset, I do not advocate having children's Sunday school at the same time as worship. While there may be pressure to do this – "my children can't possibly sit through two hours of church!" – resist! Children have no problem watching TV or playing video games for two hours at a time. The problem with having a Sunday morning church school and still trying to get everyone out in an hour is that you are depriving children (and Sunday school teachers) of the opportunity to worship with the family. When those children get old enough to make their own choices about church, they probably will not go, because they don't know how! At the same time, there will be no opportunity for adults to have educational experiences on Sunday morning with this schedule. I believe it hurts more than it helps.

Having said that, if your congregation already has a schedule of worship and children's education running concurrently, it is one of the most difficult things to change. Much as it may pain you to take children away from the church family for education, it is a change that must be attempted very slowly. There must be an attractive alternative for children, and especially their parents, to get on board with the change.

As witnessed by the Lutheran church mentioned above, Sunday morning may not be the best time for Sunday school. Many children have sports practices or games on Sunday. You may have a significant portion of your children who spend alternate weekends with another parent. Look at other times for children's Christian education – it doesn't have to be Sunday and it doesn't have to be every week.

Children in Worship Many small churches include children in the worship experience. They believe children are part of the family, and there is no "kid's table" in God's family. Those churches prefer to have children present with them in worship instead of taking them out of the room after the first hymn to go to the nursery where they are not seen and not heard. There is biblical precedence for this, of course, but some church members worry about those disciples who want to shoo the children away so the adults can hear Jesus speak without disruption or distraction. In my experience in the small church, the people who worry most about the disruption of children are their parents, who are sometimes mortified when their child speaks out or gets wiggly in church. Most people in the pews and most small church pastors are delighted to hear those happy squeals during the sermon. It reminds us as the Body of Christ that we are alive and safe and comfortable in the presence of God.

That being said, if a child is at an age where he is screaming in that piercing scream that makes stained glass shatter (you know that scream!), it is appropriate to take him to the narthex for a few minutes to calm him down. If a child is running around the sanctuary during the service and is in danger of toppling the baptismal font and hurting herself or others, it is fine if an adult gently guides her back to her seat. But generally, children in worship are fine in small congregations. Not only do they remind older members of the legacy they are leaving with the church, but it socializes children in a gentle, loving way and teaches them to be in church. When they are running around and fidgeting they are learning. Few things give me more pleasure than hearing a 4-year old belt out the Doxology or seeing the wonder on a 6-year old's face as the Communion elements are brought forward.

Of course, if you include children in worship, you have to make sure they are invited to be part of the service. Use the occasional sermon reference that a child could understand. Introduce elements in worship that not only appeal to our verbal-linguistic parts, but also to our visual and artistic selves. Have the congregation move around once in awhile. Invite a child to read the scriptures sometimes, or to lead the Call to Worship. They are part of the family too!

Many congregations, big and small, use worship bags for children to keep them occupied during those hard-to-understand parts of the service, namely the sermon. These bags are especially effective in educational ministry when they contain items that help the child to participate in worship: bookmarks to mark the hymns and the scriptures, some kind of Bible storybook or children's Bible, a coloring page or activity sheet that relates to the scriptures being preached, and perhaps some blank paper and colored pencils. Things NOT to include in worship bags: markers, crayons, scissors, food of any kind, toys that could damage pews or be noisy. Worship bags should be a tool of education, not primarily a way to keep children quiet.

Congregations who are not ready to include children fully in worship might consider taking them out for the sermon time to tell them a Bible story and do an activity, and then bring them back once the sermon is over. Other parts of the service are times when children can be taught the Lord's Prayer, the service music, how to read a hymn, how to put their offering in the plate, how to pray. It is especially important that children are present for the sacraments. These are times the community should be gathered together. Since the Communion or Eucharist is usually at the end of the service, if you have taken the children out, they should be brought back in before the sacrament begins. Children are very aware of mystery, much more than adults are. The sacraments are full of mystery and can really engage young minds and hearts.

Children's Sermons Many worship services include a time when children are called to the front for a special message just for them from the pastor or another adult. Sometimes these are connected to the adult sermon, which is a good way to engage children who will be staying to hear it, and those who will not. Sometimes they are connected to a special project the church is working on, or the church seasons, or a special guest.

I have seen children's sermons (or "time with children," or "children's worship time" or whatever you choose to call it) done well, and done very poorly.

The typical children's sermon consists of the children coming up and sitting on the steps of the chancel with the pastor, who may or may not sit with them, and listening to the pastor speak. Sometimes the pastor will say something funny to the congregation, although the children have no idea why it's funny or why everyone is laughing. The pastor speaks loudly, or speaks into a microphone, even though the children are sitting right there and can hear him just fine in his regular voice. The talk might include some questions that may or may not engage the children (and if the child answers differently than anticipated they are either ignored or laughed at), a prayer is said, and they are whisked back to their seats or off to Sunday school.

I am not completely opposed to children's sermons, although I wouldn't call them that. I think it is fine when the children have a special time only for them, and many children look forward to that. I think interpreting the day's lesson so a child can understand it is a good way to engage them in the sermon, if they are there, or in lunchtime conversation with their family if they are not. But beyond that, most children's sermons do not accomplish any educational purpose, and may do more damage than good.

Several years ago there were a spate of "Object Lessons" books that were popular tools for pastors who had no idea what to do with children during the children's sermon. The problem with these books was that they took objects and tried to use them to illustrate some abstract theological point, and young children just don't think that way! Children are concrete thinkers, and to tell them that the stuffed squirrel you brought to show them is like the man in Jesus' parable who built bigger barns is a connection they just cannot make. If you have these books on your shelf, throw them in the recycling bin. There are better things to put on your bookshelf.[27]

The main thing to remember about children's sermons is that they should be for the children, not for the congregation. Time and thought should be put into making them educational and respectful of children as people of faith and heirs of the promise. Sit with the children, don't tower over them. Talk with them, don't talk to the congregation. If the children come and sit at the front for the children's message, have their backs to the congregation; they are not on display, nor are they there for the entertainment of the adults. Listen to what they have to say; it is often profound. Enter into a holy conversation with the children.

One time I did a children's message based on the story of the Widow of Zarephath (1 Kings 17:8-16). I dressed in a long skirt with a shawl and made myself look kind of haggard (not that difficult!). I told the story in the widow's voice, and at one point asked the children if they knew what a widow was. One child, a very intense and serious 8-year old boy, spoke right up and said in a clear voice said, "Someone who's very poor." The congregation (which included a number of widows) erupted into laughter. The children were facing away from the congregation, thank goodness, but I could see the face of that little boy, who gave what he thought was a good answer, but which was greeted by laughter. He was mortified. I told him, "You're right; in my day most widows were very poor because our husbands had died, and if we had no one to take care of us, we were often left without a home or food." I recovered and he was fine, but I will never forget the look of horrified embarrassment on the face of this little boy. Children sometimes don't understand that we are laughing with them, not at them.

Church School For some reason, much of the curriculum available for purchase from denominations or Christian publishing houses assumes a large Sunday school program, even though 70-80% of congregations in mainline denominations are small. Perhaps it is because most of it is so expensive only larger churches can afford it. What does a small congregation, with five children ages 4 through 14, do with curriculum that says, "Divide your class into groups of eight...."? There are a few choices:

- Adapt printed curriculum to the small church. The problem with this is that sometimes the amount of adaptation necessary to make it work for a broadly graded group requires basically rewriting the material. It is too expensive and time-consuming to do this week after week.

- There is some curriculum written for broadly graded groups. The "One Room Sunday School" materials from Cokesbury come to mind. Other denominations have come up with either a separate broadly-graded curricula or materials that include suggestions for small groups that have a wide diversity of age. The Episcopal Church has developed curriculum especially for small congregations that is broadly graded, and available online at no cost.

- Godly Play[28] is an experiential curriculum that is based on Montessori methods and lends itself well to small churches and small groups. It is especially effective for young children, and is a way of telling Bible stories using tactile models and "I wonder" questions. Using three-dimensional figures for biblical stories, children listen and experience the story and then are able to retell it. This helps children develop a language of faith and an experience with stories of faith. The materials for Godly Play can be pricey, but this can also be a great opportunity for woodworkers in your congregation to develop the figures and materials for this ministry (they might get a little education out of it too!).

- A model of church school for children of all ages that works especially well in small congregations is the Workshop Rotation Model (WoRM).[29] This is church school using a Vacation Bible School model. The basic idea is that a Bible story is told for several weeks, each week using a different medium (art, storytelling, video, drama, music, missions, even computers and cooking). Children experience the same stories in numerous ways, which cements the story and also respects different learning styles and intelligences. In larger churches, each class meets for a different area each week. Areas of learning rotate week to week using the same story. In small churches, everyone can be together as the medium changes each week. So, for example, in the story of Moses as a baby, the first week might be a storytelling time, perhaps with a storyteller dressed as Miriam and telling the story from her perspective; the next week might be art, and children will make baskets out of reeds; the third week could be a visit from someone from the Children's Home in town and the children making a video of Moses' story to send back; the fourth week might include a children's video on the life of Moses so children can get an overview of the whole story. There is a lot of flexibility in this model, and there are several things I like about it for small churches.

>-Stories are learned well through different methods. Even children who are with another parent every other week can still get at least two weeks of the story.

>-It allows for endless outlets of creativity in the congregation.

>-It allows for teachers to teach only those areas in which they are gifted, and doesn't burn teachers out. Ask someone to lead art, and they only have to do it one time a month.

>-It allows for people in the congregation who would not consider themselves teachers to be involved. When one church I served did the story of Abraham and Sarah, I asked a couple in their 80s to dress up and tell the story. One time. They had a blast and the children loved it, and these people would never have seen themselves as Sunday school teachers.

>-If you have a larger building, you can use separate rooms for each rotation. Your art room can be equipped with art supplies, easily cleanable tables, and concrete floors, while the video room can house the TV/DVD player and have large pillows and carpet for children to relax in. Many churches paint murals on the walls to help set the scene.

-Lesson plans are available at no charge online at www.rotation.org. The website contains thousands of creative ideas that church educators have donated and from which you can pick and choose.

Vacation Bible School and other children's educational opportunities can be a great tool for education, evangelism, and ecumenism in the small church. While some congregations get frustrated that "people just use our VBS for daycare in the summer," it can be an opportunity to share the gospel with children from your church and beyond in a fun, engaging, exhausting week! You can coordinate with the other churches in town so you are offering different programs at different times, so daycare is covered (!), and children are getting quality Christian education instead of watching TV all summer.

VBS is one of those opportunities to work together with other small churches, even those of other denominations. The basic message in most VBS curricula is something akin to "Jesus loves me, this I know," or "God loves you and so do I." There is no lesson on the various understandings of what happens to the elements in Communion, or what the proper age for baptism is. There is no reason churches of a variety of denominations cannot partner together on VBS.

I also hear some frustration when VBS is seen as a tool for church growth. "We had 40 kids in VBS, and 75% of those were not from this church. Yet, not a single family has come back to the church. Our VBS was a failure." I said earlier that VBS can be used for evangelism, and that is not necessarily the same thing as church growth. In evangelism, we are sharing the gospel. I can't count the number of adults who have returned to church (or come on their own for the first time) because of the great experience they had as children's at someone's Vacation Bible School program. The seeds were planted. The VBS was a success!

Other educational programs that can involve children in the community, even if your congregation doesn't have any children regularly attending, are Christmas pageants, Christian musicals, mid-week activities, and mission projects. One United Methodist church in Wisconsin star started LOGOS – an afterschool Christian education ministry.[30] Thirty children and youth (2nd through 12th grades) are currently enrolled. The main questions to ask yourself to gauge the success of a children's educational activity are: did they learn anything about the faith, and were they welcomed with the same hospitality with which God welcomed us into God's family.

From a Clergy Spouse in a multi-cultural Presbyterian Church in California: "On our first visit to [this church] my son said, 'Mom, we belong here.' As a bi-racial 10-year old he chose this congregation before [my spouse] did. My role of church school teacher has been especially satisfying. We use the Godly Play curriculum and work with a wide age range of children, two through twelve year olds in one class. It is wonderful to see the older children helping the younger ones, each child, regardless of age, transfixed with the stories of our faith. For most of these children English is their second language, so it has been rewarding to see their growth in understanding. Sometimes even very young children can translate a story into a friend's birth language.

An American Baptist church in Massachusetts, after a three-year interim period in which they did self-evaluation and ministry goals around youth, outreach, and music, created the Harmony Youth Chorus, a weeklong music camp held at the church two or three times a year. Children from many races and ethnic backgrounds learn both musical and personal "harmony." They also housed a preschool that has attracted many children from the growing Asian population in their city.

From a Christian Church (Disciples of Christ) church in Seattle: "[This church] is a bit of a diamond in the rough: a small church that is showing compelling signs of new life, vitality, and relevance. Most striking to visitors, children almost outnumber the adults. The congregational culture is shaped by children. We are multigenerational on purpose, not by default. We truly value our elder members, always open to their knowledge, wisdom, and multi-layered life experiences. One of our greatest challenges is that in the Pacific Northwest – the least 'churched' region of the country – the predominant culture is happy to be un-tethered by the faith community. The churches literally stand in the margins. Therefore, finding ways for people to feel both intrigued and invited is a considerable undertaking! Interestingly, the children seem to be establishing the new way."

One of the exciting ministries related to education in Iowa is the Mobile United Methodist Missionaries, which takes Bible School to the people in county and city parks, town halls, wide open grassy spaces, community buildings, small churches, and trailer parks. They don't have fancy equipment, but they have what they need: Bibles, glue, markers, scissors, construction paper – "and most of all God is present with us." They have been making a difference there for over 15 years.

A small struggling United Methodist congregation in a rural Indiana, led by a retired minister, was helping his congregation to vision for the future, and asked them to remember what the church was like for them when they were children. As a result of that exercise, this congregation, made up of nearly all retired people, began to focus on ministering to children. They hold a once-a-month kids club where they prepare meals and sit and chat with the children. The kids club has grown to a dozen elementary-aged children and another dozen youth.

Youth Ministry

Even when a small church has children, they are often frustrated that there are no youth. Youth are slippery. Just when you think those 5th and 6th graders are going to be the basis of a dynamic youth program they get confirmed and leave. "How can our church possibly offer anything to young people when our pastor is old, our congregation is old, and we don't have anyone willing or energetic enough to work with youth? I certainly can't stay up all night at a lock-in!"

I will share the story of a small congregation with which I was involved, to illustrate my response to that concern, which is fairly common. At the time, this congregation had 79 members on the books, with about 35 in worship on an average Sunday. There was one teenager, a boy who attended fairly often with his mother, but they had not joined the church. There were about ten or twelve children, including about six who were entering fifth or sixth grade. Another church member and I looked at the situation and said, "We need a youth group." For two years prior to this there was a children's program called Marvelous Mondays, which included dinner, crafts, a Bible story, music, and games. After two years, they were having trouble finding adults to lead, so the program was suspended. This church member and I decided to use a weeknight format for the youth group, in case Marvelous Mondays ended up being reinstated someday, so they could meet on the same night.

As we looked at the prospect of a youth group, we went back to the basics and tried to determine what we wanted to accomplish. We were both aware of the problem that plagues many church youth ministries: once confirmation ends, rather than being the beginning of a new life in Christ it becomes a graduation ceremony from church. We thought about the meaning of confirmation and the requirements for someone to become a member of the church (this will be different in different denominations – in the Presbyterian Church, the requirements of church membership are simply being willing to profess faith in Jesus Christ). Although confirmation is usually done in 8th or 9th grade in the Presbyterian Church, there's no rule that says when it needs to happen. We thought, why not confirm them while they are younger, and then for the years we have them in church before they get a car of their own and the responsibilities of high school, they can be living into that confirmation? We took our idea to the Session (church council) and they gave us their blessing.

We began meeting every other Tuesday night (Marvelous Mondays would have to be changed to Terrific Tuesdays if they restarted) from 5 to 7 p.m. Of the six youth who were eligible, we usually had four who came regularly. We began with a game of some kind, usually just for fun. Knowing that middle school youth are very self-conscious and very gender conscious, we were careful to choose games that were safe and not embarrassing. Then we did our check-in. Instead of the usual "highs and lows," we asked, "Where did you see God this week?" and "Where was God far away from you this week?". In the beginning, they reported seeing God when the Redskins won (not that often did God appear to the Redskins!) or when they got an A on a test. But after a few weeks, they anticipated the question and came in with

"God sightings" in things such as, "I was mean to a girl in my class, and God wasn't there, but I think God was there when I apologized to her." Because they came in ready with their responses, we realized they were thinking about God during the week. We felt that if we accomplished nothing else, that was a huge success. This check-in time was followed by a short devotion that related to the theme.

Next, we did a Bible study of some kind, related to the theme of the night. We tried to be creative and everything was interactive. Then came dinner, usually prepared by a volunteer church member or parent. On those weeks when no one signed up to prepare dinner, we took them (with permission from the parents and $5) to the pizza place around the corner from the church. We usually went early and did our Bible study over dinner. These young youth did not have a problem doing that "in public," especially since it was so early that the place was rarely busy. We did encounter some teachable moments at the pizza place – such as the time a couple was huddled in the corner, way too close together, and our youth said, "That isn't really appropriate in a public place, is it," and we had a chance to talk about it.

Following dinner, we worked on some "big project," something that would carry over several weeks. Once it was illustrating a hymn; once it was planting a prayer garden on the church grounds; sometimes it was a mission project. Then we took them to the sanctuary for worship. We made a point of using a space other than the fellowship hall for worship. There we introduced them to a variety of different spiritual practices – various kinds of prayer, lectio divina, experiences with the different parts of worship, and other practices. Our rationale was that if these youth stopped coming to church as teenagers, or went off to college, we wanted to give them something to take with them so that when they were in their college dorm room and broke up with their best girl or guy and were devastated, they would have

some tools in their toolbox to use to connect with God.

For the first year of the program we focused on the "marks of membership" in the Presbyterian Church and also on who Jesus is. At the end of that year we asked them if they believed in Jesus Christ as their Lord and Savior and if they were interested in publicly professing that and joining the church. Three of them said they were ready to do that.

When we took it back to the Session to let them know we had three people ready to join the church, there was some push-back. "But they didn't learn the Catechism – I learned the Catechism in confirmation class." "But they're so young!" We reminded them that the requirement for membership was faith, not knowledge. We encouraged them to examine the youth for membership based on their faith, as is the Session's right and responsibility. When they asked them questions about their faith, those youth spoke eloquently and sincerely, and the Session was blown away!

We had an outline for six years of emphases in this program, with the first and fourth years being focused on learning about God and building our faith, the second and fifth on service to the church, and the third and sixth on service to the world. The years with similar themes would not be repeats, they would simply repeat the emphasis with different material.

This youth group was successful in that it produced faithful Christians who were thoughtful about their faith. The group was always quite small, but new youth were excited about getting to the age they needed to be to participate. The plan was not without flaws, and the Session had a hard time getting their heads wrapped around something so far outside the box, but we all had fun and learned a lot!

Some of the principles of successful youth ministry were in this process:

- Neither I nor my co-leader were young, male, or played the guitar. We were both old enough to be parents to these kids. What made them respond to us was not that we were necessarily cool, but that we loved them and respected them and listened to them. We never treated them like little kids, we treated them like human beings with something to contribute.

- We never asked for a dime from the council to do this ministry. Food was donated, and when we went out each person brought money to cover their dinner. Activities were planned intentionally so that they didn't cost anything. When a guest came in to do a project with them, the supplies were donated. We never had any complaints about that. My co-leader and I bought youth Bibles for the group, which stayed at the church, as a part of our pledge.

- We thought outside the box, starting with the very basics: What do we want to accomplish? Which structures are required and which are not? How can we make faith practical and real (relevant and authentic) to these people?

- The pastor was not involved in any of the teaching, although she was not excluded. This was a lay-led program.

- We accepted the reality that most youth will not always attend church, and tried to give them some resources that would keep them connected while they were gone.

Nancy T. Foltz, who has written the book, *Religious Education in the Small Membership Church*,[31] tells the story of her own youth in a small congregation. She was thrilled when the pastor took Nancy aside and told her that he noticed something special in her – a particularly strong faith – and encouraged her to consider going to seminary (she did not learn until many years later that he said the same thing to all of the sixth graders who went through that church!). Nancy started college, and while she was there encountered a teacher who told her that she really wasn't college material. Nan says that the combination of her mother's DNA, which made her stubborn and able to take that comment as a challenge, and the fact that she knew her small church was praying for her weekly, kept her going. She finished college and went to seminary. And through it all, her small congregation stayed with her even when she was away from them. As an adult, she may not have returned to that congregation, but she returned from college and seminary to the world, where she has made a valuable contribution. The small church's reach is much farther than the walls of their building when they send their youth off with love and with confidence and with faith.

Even if your congregation does not have a dedicated youth program, there are still many ways to have a vital and viable youth ministry. Give youth leadership opportunities in worship. Many denominations allow a young person to serve on the governing board – what a great way to develop leadership skills in a safe environment! Find opportunities for them to serve across the generations in your congregation – they are in the middle of the age spectrum, so they can help young people by teaching in Sunday school, and they can help older people with yard work or computer skills.

Another suggestion about small church youth ministry: partner with other churches in your region or in your town in activities such as youth groups or youth mission trips. Sometimes your regional office will have opportunities for the youth of many churches to work together. See if the professional educator or youth leader from a larger church might offer some time to train the youth leaders in your small church. There's no reason we can't work together.

> **The pastor of a United Methodist Church in New York State writes, "It is exciting to be in ministry where individuals of all ages can be known and their gifts valued. For example, we don't have a comprehensive youth program, but rather youth in ministry who are using their gifts as liturgists, teachers, musicians, and mission workers."**

Adult Ministry

Most adult education in small churches relies on the pastor to lead it. The pastor is, after all, trained in the Bible and in Christian education, right? Well, partly. Most seminaries do a very good job of teaching pastors how to interpret the Bible, especially for the purposes of preaching a sermon. But in many seminaries, Christian education classes are not required. The models of teaching most seminaries practice are lecture-style, which is fine some of the time, but some adults prefer a more interactive method of teaching. Sometimes the Sunday morning schedule doesn't allow the pastor to teach the adult class then. And pastors of small congregations have a lot to do! Is it possible to offer quality adult education with someone beside the pastor leading it?

In my travels, I have found a number of small churches with high quality Sunday morning adult education programs, some of which are led by the pastor and some which are led by others. In any adult education in the small church, it is important to remember who you are. Small congregations are built on relationships and on telling their story. Look for curriculum materials and Bible studies that emphasize the relational and allow people to put themselves into the story.

There are some terrific resources available that lend themselves well to being led by lay people in small churches. The Disciples of Christ publishing department,

Chalice Press,[32] offers study guides for fiction, such as *The Kite Runner, The Red Tent, The Five People You Meet in Heaven,* and others. This can be an interesting way to explore theological themes while enjoying a good novel. Another series, *Listening for God*[33], contains excerpts from well-known writers and looks at them theologically. The excerpts are each very short and work well as a way to get at biblical and theological themes in an interesting way.

Small churches should offer 101-type courses often for those people new to the faith and to the church, and those who don't want to admit they need them. Bible 101, Christianity 101, (your denomination) 101, are all ways to welcome newcomers and allow old-timers to brush up on their knowledge. These classes should allow a safe space for basic questions without embarrassment or judgment, and should be taught in a style that invites participation.

Whatever adult classes you offer, they should be welcoming to visitors and new members. It's intimidating enough walking into a small congregation, but walking into the Adult Bible Study class that has been meeting for the past 50 years is next to impossible. Make it easy!

> **From a Lutheran pastor in Chicago: "In [the church's] past, Christian Education was limited to children's classes. Now, with an emphasis on lifelong learning, weekly forums on a variety of topics are offered for adults. A monthly highlight is a "Scripture Sitcom" – believe it or not, a sitcom from the 60s or early 70s turns into a Bible study! Whatever the topic or the format, there is always great discussion at these forums.**

New Ways of Looking at Christian Education

There are all sorts of ways to turn situations and circumstances in the small church into teachable moments for people of all ages. Take advantage of the multi-generational nature of the small church and include all ages in educational events. This will keep the generations connected in ways that will have important implications in the lives of all parishioners. Tailor the needs of the people in your congregation to your educational ministry. Connect worship and education – explain the parts of worship during worship; have a class on worship; include worship in your educational experiences.

Small congregations can offer quality education and formation experiences by remembering to be who they are, building on strengths, and thinking outside that confining box of "we've always done it that way." Use the gifts and talents of your members to try innovative things. Include an educational component in all you do, from worship to mission. Strive for excellence in educational experiences for children, youth, and adults.

Here are some examples of educational excellence in small churches. You'll notice a common theme of intergenerational ministry – perfect for the small church.

> A Christian Church (Disciples of Christ)/Presbyterian united congregation in rural Iowa has a church school serving preschool-aged children through adults with class and retreat opportunities through a 29-year partnership with the United Methodist Church. The same church has cooperative educational ministries with the United Methodist and American Baptist congregations, including "Jesus and Friends" – an afterschool program for elementary students; "Fifth Quarter" – an after-game program for junior-high students; and community-wide summer Bible education.

> The pastor of a Disciples of Christ church in Texas says: " In April 2008, our congregation was the first in our region to receive the No Place for Hate Award for our work in educating our church and community to have mutual respect for all religious faiths and to honor people of all colors, genders, and sexual preference. Our church has been active since 2005 in the Coalition for Mutual Respect in which our congregation participates in a pulpit exchange with another community of faith, including Jewish, Muslim, and Christian, and a large gay and lesbian congregation."

> From the pastor of a Lutheran Church in New York State: Children are very welcome and an integral part of our worship life. Sunday School and Vacation Bible School have always been valued as a strong ministry within the congregation's life. Confirmation-age children – 7th and 8th graders – serve as ushers, acolytes, lectors, and

communion assistants, and are involved in service projects with their mentors – adult members who provide wisdom, guidance, and life experience – to help them in their faith development.

From the rector of an Episcopal church in Oregon: "Our congregation has a multi-generational Christian education program. We have twenty children ages ten and under who have inspired the older members to offer education. We discovered that while no one felt "gifted" in teaching, many people desired to be supportive of the youth and willing to offer other gifts. We provide a program one Saturday each month where adults have studied the theme of the day and then prepared their own offering of a song, a project, a storybook, or a craft in order to assist in teaching the children."

From a church leader in an Episcopal church in Chicago: "We offer child and adult formation classes between the two services under the supervision of a Formation Director. A Catechesis of the Good Shepherd class, a youth program including diocesan programs such as one which is designed for two developmentally-challenged children who are taught by parishioners, attend the Eucharist, and are included in parish-wide activities. Adults attend a forum offering a variety of educational opportunities: information on aging and caregiver resources, Bible studies, reports from delegates who have attended diocesan workshops and conventions, and discussions regarding current church issues. Usually these forums are led by the Rector, but she also invites presenters representing other community resources."

From an Episcopal priest in southwestern Michigan: "We are unique in that we have a fair number of creative types of individuals in our congregation. Several of them are involved with the theater, so we have a group called the Anglican Antics. This group has brought matriarchs from scripture alive for Mother's Day and brought patriarchs from scripture alive on Father's Day. We also have had many saints such as Queen Elizabeth and St. Francis of Assisi visit us on All Saints Sunday.

A small Lutheran church in Connecticut began an intergenerational confirmation ministry. The first year they had three sixth grade youth and seven adults in the class.

5

INSIDE THE WALLS

CARING FOR SELF AND CONGREGATION

When we were planning the themes for each summer of the Collegium, we chose five areas of ministry: Worship and Preaching, Christian Education, Pastoral Care, Mission and Outreach, and Leadership. When we got to the Pastoral Care year, we realized that although pastoral care comes naturally to many small church clergy (otherwise they probably would not enjoy small church ministry very much), self-care is more of a challenge. Being the only one on staff can fill up a schedule pretty quickly, leaving little time for self-care.

For our purposes here, we'll look at both care of others and care of self as important aspects of the life of the small church. Although much of the language in this chapter will pertain to clergy, church leaders would be well to pay attention too. You are active participants both in pastoral care of the congregation and caring for your pastor to make it easier for the pastor to stay awhile.

Pastoral Care

What are the pastoral needs of members of small churches? That might be answered by looking at some of the strengths of the small church and why people choose to be part of them. The relational nature of the small church means that every person matters. It will not do for a church member to be ill and have no one visit them or pray for them or cook them food. That is simply what one does in the small church.

People become part of the small church because they want a sense of belonging. They want to be missed if they're out of town; they want to make a contribution; they want to be part of a family. Their biological family might be far away, and their church family fills that gap. Involvement in the church takes away their sense of loneliness, and can bring a sense of fulfillment.

This need for relationship with others and with God is the main advantage small congregations have over other organizations in our society. We often don't relate to our neighbors or our coworkers in the same deep way we relate to our church family. We cannot be vulnerable in a culture where jobs are scarce and trust is even more uncommon.

Caring for people in times of difficulty is crucial to the health of a congregation. A pastor who doesn't like people has no business in the small church. He or she will never be accepted as part of the family, and will never preach an effective sermon to the people in that congregation if the people do not believe the pastor loves them and wants the best for them, much in the same way we have a hard time relating to the image of God as wrathful punisher. We relate to God as loving parent who chastises us when we need it, but does so out of indescribable love for us.

Small churches are more interested in relationships than in getting things done, in strategic planning, in finances, in almost anything else – that's why I love small churches! Letting the congregation know that you care about them is a crucial element of ministry in the small church. Beginning to develop those relationships that will lead to your "adoption" into that faith community is at least as important as preaching a good sermon.

One of the first things you will do as a new pastor of a small congregation will do is visit with those people who are in the hospital or a nursing care facility, or unable to leave their homes. The next thing you will do is visit members of the congregation. Along with that, meeting people in the community is very important to let them know that you are the new pastor, and perhaps generate some interest in visiting the church. Then, of course, there are the people who drifted away while there was not a permanent pastor in place. It's exhausting just writing about it, much less doing it!

Carl Dudley has said that small churches are larger than their membership, and large churches are smaller than their membership.

> The small church appears much stronger when measured by human relationships. If the church is defined by the number of people who know (or want to know) about one another personally, then the small church has grown. The genius of the small church is that everyone knows, or knows about, everyone else. In the small church, everyone has a place to sit and a place in the social fabric of the congregation. In larger congregations the subgroups are considerably smaller than the whole congregations of a small church. For example, the fellowship group may have thirty or forty members; a committee or a study group may have fifteen or twenty participants; a prayer cell or a sharing group may not tolerate more than eight or ten people. In larger congregations, members may know persons in one or more other groups.[34]

The implication for pastoral care, of course, is that care and support need to reach out, not only to those on the membership rolls, but to their extended families and their friends, and to people in the community who consider the church "their church," even though they do not darken the door on Sunday morning. That means the pastor will be asked to visit friends, relatives, and neighbors of church members when they are ill or in a nursing home, and preside at their funerals.

Believe it or not, difficult people also populate the small church. The reasons for this are as varied as human beings are diverse. Perhaps they are shielding themselves from being hurt again as they were by some previous pastor. Perhaps they have lost some aspect of power in the church that they had before the pastor came. Maybe on some level they want to test the pastor to see if she/he is really committed to this ministry. Or maybe their shoes are just too tight or they have an ulcer. It probably has little to do with the current pastor.

Because of the nature of the small church, not all of the people for whom you are called to provide ministry will be people you might want to be friends with in other circumstances. Practicing the spiritual discipline of seeing the face of Jesus Christ in every person you meet will help when you are called to comfort the Council member who lost his wife right after slamming you at the meeting. That might be how God feels about each one of us at times.

> **A Lutheran pastor in Iowa writes, "[Ministry in the small church] is both wonderful and painful. I have baptized the children of couples after officiating at their weddings, and attended graduations of youth I have confirmed. I have also been called to be present at the deaths of older saints or at the death of a 16-year old from complications of dystrophy. It is a holy privilege to be representing Christ at these times in people's lives."**

Care of the Pastor by the Congregation

Folks in the small church have a unique relationship with their pastor, not usually seen in larger churches. Because relationships are primary in the small church, the pastor's value in the eyes of the congregation comes from how relational he or she can be. There will be much less emphasis on the quality of the sermon or the depth of research done in preparation for the Bible study than there will be on whether or not Mrs. Jones got a visit in the hospital from the pastor.

At the same time, small church members want to love and be loved by their pastor. They want to adopt her into the family. They want him to stay a long time, long enough for them to get close to him. The congregations who do not act as if this is the case are usually the ones who have been through a long history of very short pastorates, and emotionally they are not willing to make the effort to love someone who will leave in a year or two.

This desire to love and be loved can manifest itself in unusual ways. The talk at the coffee hour will more likely be on the fact that the pastor forgot a line in the

Apostles' Creed than on the topic of the sermon. The people want the pastor to be able to show vulnerability, just as they do, in the small church. They want the pastor to be human, like them. Dudley says,

> Professional skills seem to be a barrier that separates the people from the real person of the pastor. Members of small churches have a curious method of reemphasizing the common humanity of the pastor. They enjoy his or her mistakes. They tell stories about the time the pastor stumbled into the pulpit, or made a slip of the tongue in preaching, or announced the wrong names in the midst of the funeral, or dropped the ring at the weeding, ad nauseam. To the educated pastor, who prides himself or herself on polished skills of ministry, these memories are humiliating. To the members, the stories underscore what they find most appealing about the pastor: he or she is a real person. The stories are not intended to criticize the pastor, but to bind pastor to people.[35]

Pastors of small churches learn early on that teasing is not something that should threaten, but is a way the people let you know you are accepted. It may get to be irritating, especially to your spouse, but remembering that it is a sign of inclusion in the family might make it easier to take it with a sense of humor.

Vulnerability extends not only to silly mistakes or traits that invite teasing, but also to the serious life issues that face all of us. A pastor I know was starting her first pastorate out of seminary. She had been at the church no longer than a couple of weeks when her brother died of complications from AIDS. She was devastated, of course, but also worried how her first church would react, since she had been there such a short time. She told them she would need some time off, and in the process laid her soul bare to them a little. The support she received from that church was overwhelming. It broke through that professional/people barrier and allowed them to care for her, in anticipation of the years of caring she would give to them.

Sometimes parishioners will invite you to share an activity with them which might not be your cup-of-tea, but in fact is an entrance into their lives. Jason Byassee tells the story of the parishioner in his rural North Carolina congregation (Jason's first call) who invited Jason to shoot skeet with him. Not really understanding that this did not mean killing anything, Jason said, ""Well maybe, I'm not so sure." Jason continues, "He let it go, and never offered again. All he meant was he'd fire clay disks in the air and we'd blast 'em. It'd have been an occasion to talk, get to know each other, even learn about what our lives outside of church were like. He noticed my hesitation, even discomfort, and let it go. I never had that opportunity back."[36]

Other small church pastors have mentioned coming home to find the freezer of the parsonage stocked with a side of beef, or fresh vegetables from parishioners' gardens waiting in a basket on their doorstep. Who wouldn't want to serve a small church when people are as loving as this?

Although not all people in the small church are as open and loving as these examples suggest, it may be that the same intense emotion is what drives both the giving ones and the grumpy ones: a deep love of their church and of one another. How they view the pastor may be as savior or as intruder or as fellow traveler on the journey. Some of that depends on how carefully the pastor walks in the first few months of the pastorate.

Care of the Pastor by the Pastor

Pastoral care of a small congregation, with no help, can be draining, especially for an introvert who gains energy from being alone. It can be lonely and thankless to be the pastor of a small church, especially in a small town away from everything. A huge issue for clergy of small congregations is self-care. Unless the pastor is willing to set boundaries and be mindful of her own health, it is easy to work too much, expect too much of yourself and your parishioners, and burn everyone out. Of course, some people in the congregation think pastors only work on Sundays!

It is the pastor's responsibility to manage self-care. No one else will do it for you. When I work with Pastor Search Committees I always urge them to keep an eye out to make sure the new pastor is taking enough vacation and continuing education time, and not trying to do everything herself. But a search committee cannot know how many hours you put in at home, and how many vacations you cancel because of a pastoral emergency – vacations you will not get back. It is the nature of pastoral ministry that things come up unexpectedly, but it really is all right to take an extra day off the next week when you've been up all night with a grieving family and then have to plan and carry out the memorial service.

In the same way small congregations cannot provide programming to meet every need of every member of the congregation and those outside it, neither can a pastor do everything and do it well. Clergy in small congregations generally like the variety of work – they are generalists rather than specialists (as they would be in a large church). But having all or most of the work on the shoulders of the pastor can be burdensome in weeks where there is a funeral or unexpected pastoral care emergency.

Interestingly, although we found that in most areas small church life in different denominations is very similar, it varies by denomination in self-care for clergy. Some denominations insist on continuing education – the United Methodist Church requires a certain number of Continuing Education Units (CEUs) per year for pastors. Others require time and money for continuing education as part of the package. But in some denominations this is not required, or even encouraged, since the amount of money available is either non-existent or so paltry it would barely cover one night away. The Episcopal Church does a good job of encouraging its priests to have a pastoral counselor and/or spiritual director.

The areas of self-care that should all be taken seriously by pastors are:

Spiritual health – This may be the most difficult self-care practice for pastors of small congregations. Many pastors have a difficult time worshipping when they are leading worship. Do you have daily time for prayer and Scripture reading that is not related to your sermon? Do you have particular practices in which you engage that bring you closer to God? If you neglect personal spiritual practices that feed your soul, you will be in danger of burnout, loss of focus, and setting a poor example to those congregants whom you urge to read the Bible and pray daily. Perhaps having a spiritual director or spiritual friend – outside of the congregation – will help to hold yourself accountable for your spiritual health.

Physical health – I know what church potlucks are like. I know it takes a lot of time sitting at a computer or commentaries to come up with a sermon. I know it takes time to exercise when your day is already full, and it's easier to grab a Big Mac than fix dinner on committee meeting nights. Find fun ways to get exercise – walk the dog or do a pastoral visit while walking the mall. Get a gym buddy who will keep you accountable for going to Curves three times a week. Cook healthy meals - some of the small-church pastors I have met are terrific cooks! Let your congregation know you are trying to lose a few pounds, and make sure there are some healthy choices at those potlucks. What are you doing to promote your physical health, which will also impact your other areas of health?

Intellectual health – Many towns have a clergy study group that meets weekly to discuss the lectionary passages. Do you receive a study leave allowance? Use it! If you don't get one, consider asking your board for a continuing education/study leave allowance in next year's package. It will only benefit the congregation when you are up to date on the latest resources and scholarship. If that is not possible, read! Your seminary may be willing to send books to you on loan. In the Presbyterian Church, clergy have a book allowance as part of their terms of call; this is for the intellectual health of the pastor, not to buy study books for the adult education class!

Relational health – Do you keep up relationships with friends outside of the church and town in which you serve? They can be valuable resources when you have an issue in the congregation and cannot (MUST NOT) discuss it with a church member, or even with a neighboring pastor. Do not sacrifice your family to your ministry. Many clergy I know have a date night scheduled once a week with their spouse or partner, which is a sacred time together.

The Episcopal Church's Church Pension Fund developed a kind of retreat on self-care called CREDO,[37] which has now been started in the Presbyterian Church (USA). This is an eight-day retreat which clergy and lay professionals are randomly selected to attend, which explores areas of physical, vocational, financial, and spiritual health. It has proven very effective for many who have attended. Most of the cost is paid by the Church Pension Fund, in an effort to promote health among church workers.

Here are some examples of healthy behaviors and struggles from pastors of small congregations:

> My practices include daily prayer and meditation, study, yoga, and walking; periodic guided and silent retreats, journaling and fasting, group spiritual direction, and clergy gatherings of various sizes and affiliations; wide range of reading from theology to pop self-help to novels. I attend regional and national conferences on a regular basis, most recently a series based upon the work of Parker Palmer. The life of our denomination offers opportunities to support the health and effectiveness of clergy through the Board of Ordained Ministry where I serve as division chair for continuing education and spiritual formation. An outgrowth of my graduate degree in staff development, I enjoy training, coaching, mentoring, and leading retreats. Important to both of us, [my husband] and I share prayer, study, hiking, gym time, music, sailing, healing practices. We also traveled on pilgrimage to Scotland and Iona last year.

An Episcopal priest in Massachusetts writes: "The biggest factor in all of these areas is my own attention and intention, which fluctuates. I am a spiritual director to four very different individuals. I meet monthly with my spiritual director and clericus, take an annual ten-day retreat, and walk on the Appalachian Trail and around town with my dog and friends. I am learning and playing the violin, play in a canasta group, practice Tai Chi, and enjoy two friendship groups that focus on contemplative prayer and creative ministry as well as being a safe place to talk and be. I also have a year-old granddaughter with whom I can act like a kid and have a lot of fun."

From a United Methodist Church pastor in Wisconsin: "I am a sister in the Order of St. Luke and I take my vows very seriously, which include a prayer and study life that brings me great comfort. I have participated in the Walk to Emmaus communities and will serve as an assistant Spiritual Director for this fall's walks. Tuesday nights I participate in an ecumenical Bible Study on prophecy, and on Wednesday mornings I am involved in an ecumenical women's Bible study. I am the Circuit Leader for our circuit. Each week, on

Thursday morning the clergy meet in a Wesleyan-based small group, where we share the initial questions of 'How is it with your soul?' I go to the gym three times a week and feel very good about the program and the friendships I have made while working out with the town's women. I have attended workshops on preaching, pastoral counseling, and spiritual growth. In order to keep our marriage strong, Harry and I have established 'date nights' and most every day join one another in taking the dog for walks. To stay connected with the community I am part of the Ecumenical Ministerial Society, which also deals with things like the local Food Pantry, and other ecumenical ministries in our town."

From the pastor of a United Church of Canada congregation in Toronto: "I learned early on that physical exercise is crucial to my well-being. In the summer I am an avid cyclist and in the winter an almost fanatical curler. I also attend the gym two to three times per week and walk as much as I can in God's good and holy world. I find taking care of myself physically refreshes my being and gets me out of my head. I have a large circle of friends of all sorts of ages and interests, most of them who have nothing to do with the church, who keep me balanced. I have a prayer life that keeps me connected to my God, and a lot of clergy friends to debate theology with over a beer. Lately I decided I was bored with the lectionary, so have challenged my congregation to identify biblical characters and faith issues that intrigue/puzzle/concern them and I have found the study this requires to prepare worship a theological and scholarly challenge that I miss from my student days."

An Episcopal priest from Oregon writes: "The CREDO workshop was extremely helpful in setting up my current program of maintaining my health and spiritual well-being. I have a spiritual director I visit once a month and I make a weeklong spiritual retreat to a monastic retreat center once a year. Physical exercise is a balance between outdoor recreation of hiking, kayaking, and running. The church provides me with a sports club membership, which I currently use to train for a half marathon. Intellectually, I rely on colleagues to discuss the latest books we are reading. As for relational health, I live near enough to all my dearest family and friends that I make a point of making an overnight visit to someone once a month."

Another Episcopal priest, this one from Arkansas: "As most pastors experience, life is very busy. A small church does not mean there is a small amount of work to be done – on the contrary! Taking care of one's self when time can be so precious becomes an intentional act. Physically I care for my body by walking and by lifting weights each week. Both are interests I share with my husband. Recently I have started music lessons, learning to play a mountain dulcimer. Intellectually I read as much as I can, both fiction and reference; and I am a computer 'nerd' and enjoy the numerous benefits of our technological age. My family and I maintain healthy relationships with our travel, both domestic and internationally, dining together, and love of the cinema. Our adult children are currently working and in graduate school or college. Spiritually, my self-care is actualized through prayer, working with a spiritual director and diocesan programs."

Care of Volunteers

No one stays in a small church expecting to be anonymous. Likewise, no one stays in a small church thinking they won't be involved. There is much to do and the workers are few in the small church. There will be people in the church whose life revolves around it, but others who are juggling small children, aging parents, jobs, illness, and mobility issues that make it difficult for them to be so committed.

We'll discuss lay leadership at more length in the chapter on Leadership, but we touch on it here because it is important for pastoral leaders in the small church to remember that just like pastors, volunteers can get burned out too. They may not be able to tell you they are overworked, but it will inevitably show in their attention to projects and their demeanor.

Well-trained volunteers are confident volunteers. Asking someone to read Scripture in front of the congregation can be intimidating for someone not used to speaking in public, especially if it happens to be Pentecost Sunday and they have to stumble through all those odd-sounding tribe names! It's wonderful for volunteers to be asked to participate in the worship service, but practice with them first if they need it. The same goes for committee work, or work on the board.

Take the time to train people for ministry so they know what to expect when they agree to serve. Many who accept a leadership role on the Council or Session or Vestry see that role as similar to being on a Board of Directors, rather than being the spiritual leaders of the church.

Make sure in your congregation that the assumption is NOT that the pastor will do everything and the board members will do everything else. Just because someone is not actively serving on the board does not mean they cannot chair a project or help with the Food Pantry. "We're all in this together" is the preferable attitude to "we elected you to lead, so you do it!"

If you find yourself lacking volunteers for a particular ministry, maybe it's time to evaluate whether that ministry is still valuable to the congregation or the community. If there is no energy around an activity, maybe that's the sign that it's time to suspend it for awhile. The same goes for service on the board. If year after year you have to beg, bribe, and shame people into allowing their names to be put up for a board position, perhaps the size of the board needs to be cut, or they need to evaluate why people are reluctant to serve. Do the meetings run excruciatingly long? Is there conflict every month? Are board members expected to do everything in the church? These may be problems to address.

Finally, if you ask someone to do something, make sure they know what they're getting into. Don't try to sweeten it and make it seem like it won't take any time or effort. And if they say no, respect that. The last thing you want is someone in charge of a project who doesn't want to do it. Consider asking people for shorter-term commitments: organizing one potluck rather than chairing the Fellowship Committee; co-teaching a six-week Sunday school class rather than signing on for the whole year.

Working with volunteers can be difficult, although I think the commitment level of volunteers in the small church is much higher than in a larger church because they know that if they don't do it, no one else will be able to do it for them. Pastoral leaders should keep in mind the pastoral and spiritual care of volunteers. They are the backbone of the small church.

The Value of Funerals and Baptisms

When I mention to groups that small congregations are the best at funeral ministry, there is often nervous laughter. I guess they think I'm referring to the gray-haired make-up of many small churches. But I'm serious about that. When someone in the small church dies, or when someone from the community wants to use the church building for a funeral or memorial service, the small church kitchen brigade gathers and puts on a feast, filled with hospitality and abundance, like you've never seen! The leftovers – and there are always plenty of leftovers – go home with the bereaved, along with the love and prayers of the preparers.

The ministry provided by the members of the congregation at funerals, baptisms, weddings, or prayer vigils is vitally important in the small church. Those kitchen ladies may not know it, but they are offering pastoral care to the community along with the fried chicken, potato salad, and casseroles. They are being allowed into the most intimate moments of a person's life, those times of crisis and stress that are usually reserved only for immediate family.

Special events that occur in the church building are also golden opportunities for showing the world outside the church what church is really about. These are times when many unchurched people enter the church, perhaps for the first time since they were children, perhaps for the first time ever. The church has gotten a pretty bad rap in the media in the past 25 or 30 years. But if all someone knew about the church was what they saw on TV, they would think "church" was synonymous with being judgmental, with only being interested in money, with extreme fundamentalism, with burning the Koran and picketing military funerals. But what the small church presents to attendees at funerals, baptisms, and weddings, can be church the way it was meant to be – loving, caring, nurturing, a safe place where it's ok to be vulnerable and share your feelings. The media has stopped showing this side of the church very much. It is the greatest strength of the small church, so when we are presented with those opportunities, we should rise up and show our best face. Although I understand the theological and practical reasons for not allowing non-member baptisms and weddings, and perhaps even funerals, I think the opportunities for pastoral care and even evangelism outweigh the concerns. They might be our best shot at showing the love of Jesus Christ to the world.

Following are some more examples of small congregations and pastoral care. You may notice some overlap in these examples with other areas of ministry, which is really how the small church works. The life of ministry in the small church is not compartmentalized, but is all there together, just as her people are one single cell of caring.

> **More from that same pastor on why he loves ministry in the small church: "In a word, family. Members in a small church know each other. During a recent baptism one of our senior members, sitting close to the family, was asked if they were a grandparent. 'We're all that baby's grandparents!' was the immediate, and true, reply. This is expressed personally in a congregation that is truly caring and supportive of me. During some periods of ill health, pulpit support was immediate and concern was never 'When can you get back to work?,' but 'How can we help you get better?' This is a fun congregation to be in!"**

> **From the pastor of a United Church of Canada congregation in Manitoba: "This is the first congregation in 28 years of small church ministry which has had a local emergency fund. I've used it to provide transients with a meal, a worker with steel-toed boots for his job, swim passes to the local pool, a trip to the area camp, etc. [Our town] is close enough to the city that many of its young adults have been able to stay in the community while finding work. This has led to larger family clusters than in other small churches I have served."**

> **The pastor of a Christian Church (Disciples of Christ)/Presbyterian**

united congregation in rural Iowa: "[What we call] 'Parish Deacons' – Stephen Ministry-trained 'deacons' provide primary Christian care and support to congregational members and friends through nine parish groupings."

From an Anglican Church in a small town in Ontario: "One thing that is unique at [our church] is the presence of an active Stephen Ministry group. This is a specially trained lay pastoral team who walk with people through times of illness, death of a loved one, family crisis or other personal troubles. The second thing I would say that is unique about [this church] is that they truly care for and love one another. It is the closeness of these relationships that has made them an open and welcoming community and has given strength to some significant outreach programs."

The rector of an Episcopal Church in Alaska writes: "I came to [this congregation] from a large and prosperous cathedral congregation in the Midwest. I thrive on the contact with individuals which the smaller congregation allows. My pastoral care duties are frequent and complex. Many members of the congregation are related to one another by birth-family or marriage. This network of relationship demands careful attention. In the summer, invariably, I am called upon to respond to the needs of transient workers who come to this area to work in the fishing industry. Many of them find themselves stranded here and without the means to get back to their homes in the lower 48 states. Medical and psychiatric care are limited, at best. Emergency cases must be taken by air to major cities that are at least two hours flying time away. My pastoral care seems to be possibly more critically important than it would be in a larger urban setting."

From a young pastor with a young family pastoring a Disciples of Christ church in northern California: "Ministry in the smaller church allows me to know the people I serve. In many ways, smaller churches make a big difference in the life of their members. Being in a small rural community, people know me, even if they do not participate in the life of the congregation. Area youth feel free to stop by or talk or to 'hang out' at the pastor's house. An example: In July 2005, a neighbor who does not attend [the church] but who is familiar with our ministry asked if I could provide safe shelter to her teenage son, since she could not. Her son ended up living with me and my family for four months. This was a positive life-changing event not only for the youth, but for me personally as well as other church and community members who saw what was happening. Before he moved out of my home and out of the community, the teenager joined the church as a symbolic gesture of the family he had found there.

From a pastor in Missouri: "We have a program in our Pastoral Care Committee called a shepherd program. Each of twelve shepherds has various sheep they are responsible for. Sheep receive greeting cards, visits, and calls from the shepherds and even other sheep. It is amazing to me the number of times as pastor that I visit or call on a person in need and find that a shepherd has already visited or called."

6

OUTSIDE THE WALLS

MISSION AND OUTREACH

The first indicator of health in a small congregation is whether anything is being done for those outside the walls of the building. Conversely, a sign of serious disease in a congregation is that the members spend most of their energy on one another. Many small churches do a great job of taking care of themselves – they are quick to fill the freezer of a member who has experienced a loss or had a baby; they check on one another when someone is absent from church for a while; they often care deeply for their pastor and make sure she or he is supplied with vegetables from their gardens and cake on a birthday. This is all commendable. But unless there is an intentional effort to love neighbor as well as self, the church is likely headed for problems.

Can We Make a Difference?

When I worked as a church educator, every year I would tell the children about the One Great Hour of Sharing offering, an ecumenical mission opportunity that happened during the Lenten season, where children received little banks to save their coins, and all the boxes were received during the Easter service. I told them the stories of some of the people who had been helped with One Great Hour of Sharing offerings. One year a little boy asked how his pennies would be able to help someone whose house had been destroyed by a flood. I explained that his own box of coins might not be enough to help, but when we combined it with the boxes of the other children in our church, and in other Presbyterian churches and then other churches of all kinds, it added up to a lot of money, and was a big help to a lot of people.

The same is true for mission in the small church. Small congregations cannot have a portfolio of 50 organizations they help with their mission dollars and their already tired hands. Usually a small church can do one or two mission activities a year and do them well. Some congregations I know try to have a "Mission of the Month," but that may be too ambitious for many small churches. It will be more sensible to take on a couple of hands-on projects and put a lot of energy and effort into them, striving for excellence. One small congregation can make a huge difference, as you'll see in some of the examples presented at the end of this chapter.

Certainly there are other mission efforts that would be secondary to the one or two big ones; giving money to denominational causes, for example, is not a major mission project in and of itself, in the same way hosting a weekly free meal for the homeless might be. These "hands-off" mission activities are valuable and are especially helpful for people who just cannot participate in a meaningful way with mission that involves presence and physical activity. It is important, though, to look at the lines in the budget and do a careful analysis of those organizations you support, to make sure there is still a viable connection between the mission opportunity and the congregation. Sometimes those line items continue in the budget for years and no one remembers why they are there.

It is noteworthy that many small congregations end up near the top of their regional office's list of mission giving, when it is calculated on a per capita basis. The percentage of giving per member is often much higher in small churches than in large churches. Celebrate these accomplishments – small churches can make a difference!

Understanding the Context of Ministry for Mission

In my experience, the most important part of deciding on mission activities is to bloom where you are planted. Look at the context of your ministry and celebrate who you are and what you are doing. Then begin to dream about what you could do to show the love of Christ to those in need.

It may seem obvious, but some congregations make the mistake of trying to replicate the mission of a congregation in a very different context, ensuring frustration. Take a close look at the community in which you are located. What has changed? What are the needs? Who are the anonymous people in the community who are forgotten by the social service agencies? What can your congregation do to help?

Small churches seem to prefer mission in their own communities, where they can see it at work. In recent years there has been less of an emphasis on foreign mission as congregations have realized there is plenty of need at home. Explore the social service agencies in your community – in what ways can the congregation be supportive of their work? Develop relationships with the staff of these agencies, so that when there is a particular need, they will contact you. Small church members will give generously of time and money to something tangible, something where they can see the good they are doing.

I've encountered an urban pastor who saw a need for something for young people of the community to do to keep them out of trouble, and started a ministry for them. He also began a "Stop the Violence" mentoring program for troubled youth in the community. A congregation in a struggling small town setting might offer computer classes to help out of work residents to increase their skills so they are better able to find work. But starting an English as a Second Language ministry in a town that has no non-English speaking residents is obviously not a good use of mission energy. Jesus' caring ministries were always offered in the context of need.

Healthy and vital small congregations are aware of their environment and the needs of their communities, and respond to those needs. They are known in their communities for the work they do. When the question is asked, "If this church were to close, would anyone notice?" these congregations can name mission activities that are relevant and effective ministries in their town or neighborhood. They are known by outsiders for the mission work they do.

It's true that resources are often scarce in the small church, but it's also true that when the need is clear and pressing, small church folks will rush to help. In addition, there may be grant money available for special projects. Check with your denomination for suggestions.

Take time to listen to the community; you will learn the needs, hopes, and dreams of your neighbors, and find opportunities for ministry and mission.

Ecumenical and Integrated Ministry

Many small congregations have found that ecumenical ministry helps them to put together the numbers needed to tackle a larger project than they could do on their own. Once we get beyond the fear that other churches will "steal" our members, very effective ministry can occur. Denomination and theological perspective are usually irrelevant when it comes to serving the needs of the poor or hurting in our community. If we are trying to reclaim our roots in the early church, denominational divisions would dissolve.

In the small churches I visited, I have witnessed many examples of ecumenical mission and education activities. With large numbers of small churches coexisting in a small town or rural area, it makes good sense to combine forces on some ministries. Our language is basically the same, and our issues as small congregations are the same. A small Christian congregation and a small Jewish gathering probably have more in common than a small and large congregation in the same denomination. Why can't we offer support to one another, and increase our effectiveness? Ecumenical ministry can model cooperativeness to the community and to church members.

Personally, I'm not quite ready to advocate for one Christian denomination, but it wouldn't be the worst thing. Perhaps that is where we are headed. In the meantime, it wouldn't hurt to increase our understanding of other denominations and other religions.

Welcoming the Stranger

Just about every small church will tell you they are welcoming and friendly. The truth is that many believe they are friendly because they are friendly to one another. They may not be so welcoming to visitors. It's easy to live in the vacuum of the church and not really know how you are perceived by others. I enjoy walking into small churches as a visitor to see how I am greeted. It is not a bad idea for you to ask an outsider to do that and report back to you about how easy the church is to find, how accessible the church is, how they were greeted, how they understood the service.

A couple of times I have had the privilege of visiting small towns with the assignment of finding out how people in the town see the church. I go into shops and ask directions to the church, then ask what they know about that church. The results have been interesting. In a town of about 600 residents, I asked where St. Mary's Episcopal Church was, the responses were, "Is that the Catholic church?" and "I don't think we have an Episcopal church." Looking for the Methodist church on the outskirts of town, the responses were, "Oh, I know that pastor – he's a member of the Kiwanis Club – he's nice," and "I think the pastor serves on the Volunteer Fire Department." What is the reputation of your church in town? Do people see the church as the church that is dying, or the church that does that great mission project every year? Are they the church where all the people with money go, or the church that has a great Vacation Bible School? I hope they're not known by people in their town as the church that is always fighting over something or other, or the church that went through that scandal a few years ago. Or maybe it would be even worse if people said, "What church? I never heard of that church."

We already discussed the worship service and worship bulletins. What does your worship service convey to outsiders? Little things like the font in the bulletin and the quality of the printing can reveal the church as stuffy, old fashioned, or tired, instead of modern and striving for excellence.

Look at your church facilities – do they long for the 1960's? Is the nursery clean? Can you be proud of your building and grounds? Is the church accessible to those with mobility issues? Would you want to visit this church with your young children or aging parent? We also know that a huge sanctuary that is empty can be intimidating to visitors, just as a sanctuary that is full will send the message that the visitor is not needed.

How open is your congregation to welcoming the stranger – someone different from you? It is a good practice to think about where you might draw the line; this would be an interesting discussion to have, to be very frank about what kinds of things you would accommodate. Ask yourself if you would welcome:

- Children (and if so, what accommodations will you make for them in worship and other activities)?

- The elderly (is your building on two levels, with the sanctuary at ground level and the Fellowship Hall where everyone gathers for social time down a steep flight of stairs)?

- Teenagers (even if they wore jeans and a t-shirt, or had pink hair, or a nose ring)?

- Someone from another ethnic group (and what changes in music or preaching would you be willing to make)?

- Someone whose first language is not English (and will you print some copies of the bulletin in their language if they are regular attenders)?

- A same-sex couple?

- Someone with a visual or hearing impairment (and will you provide a large-print bulletin and hymnal, or a hearing assistance device)?

- Someone with mental or emotional challenges?

- Someone with a lower socioeconomic standing than those in the congregation?

- Someone who smells bad?

- Someone who is homeless?

You can add to the list. I had one congregation tell me that frankly, they would accept most of those things, but someone with a lower level of education would have a hard time fitting into their church. You may not be able to positively accommodate all of these people, especially since some "fixes" are expensive (elevators, hearing devices, etc.), but it is something for which your church can struggle, remembering that we do not own our churches; they are places for the people of God to gather and find welcome.

Another important welcoming behavior occurs after someone decides to join your congregation. In the small church, one person or family can have a huge impact on the congregation. Instead of being one of 250, they are one of 35, so their contribution is that much more important. Each new member brings the history of their own individual faith journey, ideas from other churches, gifts and talents, and hopes and needs. How willing are you to change the way things have been done to respect and take seriously the ideas of someone new? What if they sit in your pew? What if they want to help in the kitchen? What if they want to start a liturgical dance group? How will your congregation react? No one will be involved in the life of the church if they feel their voice is not heard, and they are seen only as a new contribution to the offering plate or someone to teach Sunday school. We all want our contribution to be valuable and valued.

At a workshop one time, the leader asked the question of small church folks, "What is the length of time, on average, that it takes for someone to drive into your parking lot, get out and go into the church building, stay for worship, join the church, and is asked to teach Sunday school?" Someone immediately shouted, "Same day!" Everyone thought that was funny, but it may be more true than we like to admit. There is plenty of literature on new member assimilation that says you have to get a new member involved in something significant within six months, or one month, or two weeks, depending on the writer, or you will lose them. I don't have a magic formula, but getting someone involved in the small church is usually not a problem. Small churches are usually a bit too eager.

It helps to look at hospitality not as welcoming the stranger so the load of everyone else will be eased, but welcoming the stranger with open arms of love and acceptance in the same way God welcomed each one of us into the family of faith. Look at hospitality as a spiritual practice, rather than what I call "Dracula Evangelism," we need some new blood around here!

Getting Outside the Walls

All that being said, it is much less likely these days that people will flock to your church, as was the case in the 1950s and 1960s, when all you had to do was man the doors and greet the newcomers. It is imperative that folks in the congregation face up to the dreaded "E" word – evangelism. The connotations associated with evangelism are often off-putting to church members, conjuring up visions of knocking on the doors of strangers and handing out tracts, or standing on the street corner with a Bible preaching hellfire and damnation. Most denominations have learned that those methods aren't very effective.

Instead, church members can look at evangelism as simply sharing something that has been life-giving for you with your friends. You'd do it if it were a new over-the-counter cold medicine that gets rid of a cold in 24 hours, or a new restaurant that has terrific Italian food. The overwhelming majority of people who become members of churches do so because they were invited by a friend or relative.[38] That's relational ministry, and we know small church folks know how to do that.

After checking to make sure your church will indeed be welcoming, invite friends to a fellowship meal or invite them to help hand out food to the homeless. Better yet, as you get to know them personally, talk about what your church can help them with something important to them and talk about what your church and your faith means to you. You don't have to be able to quote Scripture (that might have the opposite effect), or have a four-point canned statement of faith, simply tell your friends about what is important to you about being a Christian. Tell your story.

There are people in your community who have never been inside a church (except perhaps for the occasional funeral, baptism, or wedding). There are few things I can think of that are more intimidating than walking into a place that has unusual customs and language, and a common history that the visitor does not know. There is a whole generation or two of people who claim to be "spiritual but not religious," which means they are suspicious of institutions and prefer to find their faith in the forest or on their own.

Dennis Bickers recommends going back to the Acts 2 church, which, like the Christian church today, existed in an environment hostile to Christianity. This is the church where people gathered together for prayer and fellowship, shared meals, and shared their lives.

> The model used so successfully in the first century is the model that is most appropriate for the small church today. In healthy small churches people are brought to faith in Christ by being brought into the family of faith. Although it does not reach large numbers of people at one time, it is very effective. An unhealthy small church will not effectively reach out in this way, because it's more concerned with its level of comfort than with outreach, but a healthy church will be excited about the prospect of seeing new people come to Christ and into the church. A healthy church will look for ways to establish relationships with unchurched people, and they'll seek opportunities to share both their faith and their church with their new friends. Such relationships will become doors through which people can enter into a personal relationship with Jesus Christ.[39]

I have found that young people today are drawn to the church differently than the Baby Boomers. This generation does not come to faith through listening to sermons and reading the Bible as much as they do through hands-on mission – doing something. This group has no interest in writing a check for overseas mission; they want to do the work and see the faces of the people they are helping. For fifteen years I took groups of high school youth to workcamps in the summer. During the early stages of planning the trips, I would ask them to tell me why they wanted to go to workcamp (it was, after all, a week sleeping in a sleeping bag on the floor of a school and long, hot days spent repairing homes). Their responses were fairly consistent over the years: to get away from home for awhile, to get the community service hours needed to graduate, and to be with my friends. On the trip home from the workcamp experience, I asked them to write a paragraph or two about their experience, and the responses were profound. They talked about how their faith was developed through the work, and how they experienced Jesus while looking into the tear-filled eyes of the resident who now had a wheelchair ramp and could leave her home to get to the doctor. They saw the fruits of their labors, and found Christ in working for others.

This is a lesson for the small church, and for all churches, because all churches are failing at attracting young people. Think of some ways to open mission projects to the community for a short-term, no commitment to join, experience. Do it in the name of Jesus Christ, don't try to hide it, but avoid preaching or nagging them to come to church. You might be surprised at the results of these efforts. Young people want a faith, they are just looking for it in different places and different ways than earlier generations did.

Carl Dudley says that young people and older people all want to get to the same goal – a faith in a higher being. But the two groups are on parallel tracks: older people are seeking faith through religious organizations, and younger people are getting their faith from the media and a variety of religions. It is those events that cross those two parallel lines, events such as funerals and weddings and mission projects, which allow one group to see into the world of the other. And it is the times that young people come to the church (for a wedding or funeral) that the church needs to show its best face. Dudley would tell the story of his five adult children, who were on both sides of this new mentality about the church. The older two, he said, were churchgoers – one was a pastor and one was an elder. The middle child was seeking religion through some non-Christian methods. The younger two had rejected the church – but when it came time for one of them to get married, he asked his father to stand with him because he wanted the presence of the church there.[40]

The examples of mission and outreach in small churches across North American are numerous. May these stories inspire your congregation!

> **The pastor of a Lutheran congregation in rural Indiana says: "The unique ministry [our church] has developed is a ministry of healing. People who attend here have come from various church backgrounds that were suppressive, and they are seeking a grace-filled relationship with the Lord. Reasons people seek out the fellowship [of this church] are various, but three issues are prevalent: divorce, re-marriage, and spiritual abuse. I take comments regularly that people who are seeking a second chance in their spiritual life or relationships often visit and stay."**

> **From the member of an Episcopal church in Chicago: "We feed**

people. The feeding takes many forms – our hunger relief ministry, our parish fellowship meals, and our spiritual formation. We have been approached to become a Jubilee Parish because of our twenty-five year program of delivering end-of-day perishable food from a local grocer and a coffee house to soup kitchens and food pantries three times a week. We also supply non-perishable items to another local food pantry weekly. All parishioners are encouraged to bring a can on Sunday (B.A.C.O.N.) and these are brought to the altar for a blessing. Our Rector asked the Vestry to instigate discernment meetings to determine our direction as a parish in the future, and it was determined that adopting the first Millennium Development Goal of eradicating hunger would be an appropriate undertaking for our parish. We invited other parishes in the diocese to join us in our commitment to this project, and church leaders will be presenting this idea to other religious establishments in our community."

From the pastor of a United Methodist church in Minnesota: "We have a strong tradition of missions in our church. We hold Mission Conferences from time to time, and I have led two short-term volunteer-in-mission teams (consisting partly of church members) to Uganda in East Africa. We have had members travel to Africa and Jamaica on similar mission trips three other times during my tenure, and have combined with area churches on a youth mission trip to inner city Chicago. Locally we take a turn serving a Saturday meal for homeless and disadvantaged persons at a church in a larger community every year, and support a variety of other ministries. This congregation also owns and operates a ball field, sponsoring fast-pitch softball teams for youth each summer. The field includes an operating concession stand and lights for evening games. Though the community has only two streets (it is formed at a crossroads) we sponsor a large 4th of July parade every year that generally draws a few thousand people, followed by a lunch (fundraiser) at the church. The church plans and runs the parade every other year, alternating with the community center (though many of the same people are in both groups). There are no other churches in this community."

From a United Church of Canada clergy spouse from Ontario: "I would describe my recent role as one of raising awareness of social justice issues. I have spoken about the global problem of human trafficking during worship, planned letter writing campaigns for Amnesty International and organized a Ten Thousand Villages Festival sale as ways of educating and engaging the congregation in social justice work."

A United Church of Christ church in Iowa reports: "Part of the reason we have had few visitors may be that we have no building. Because of one of our core values, which is mission, we did not want to tie up our assets in a building which, for a group of about 40 people, would be quite a burden. We worship in a room of the chapel building at the local college which is very comfortable but not very visible."

"We take a trip every summer to a Native American reservation where we have friends, and we send them Christmas clothes and winter heating money. We serve two meals a month at the Catholic Worker house, and a free dinner at the county building once a month. We usually have an annual fundraiser for the Central Iowa AIDS Project."

The pastor of a Lutheran church in Pennsylvania writes: "From the start, [this church] has been blessed with a clear vision and great hope for the future. In June of 2006, while I was on a much-needed sabbatical, the congregation went ahead and purchased 25 acres in a great location. In March of 2008 we broke ground for the new building, then moved in and celebrated the dedication in fall of 2009. When we were faced with financial constraints midway through the building process, we chose to delay completion of the sanctuary and get the multi-purpose area and food bank storage up and running first – because this would best serve our mission of outreach to the community. We are excited about being able to provide a permanent home for the local ecumenical food pantry. We have also been excited about the ways we can make good use of our

25 acres. For the past three summers – even before we broke ground for the building – we have grown sweet corn and potatoes to give away to local food ministries. We have also been able to use the land to raise wheat and soybeans to support the building fund."

The pastor of a United Church of Christ church in California writes: our congregation is small but finds ways to do the things we feel called to. We helped found the local Interfaith Coalition for the Homeless; we work with a nearby Episcopal Church at their Tuesday worship and free meal program. Through that ministry I discovered Ecclesia Ministries, an international ecumenical group dedicated to street church – bringing hospitality, healing, prayer, and celebration to our un-housed sisters and brothers. Each week, on Sunday afternoon, we hold street worship on an old downtown bridge. Following the service we serve sandwiches, fruit, hot coffee, and sometimes a hot meal because the people are often hungry and cold."

From a Presbyterian church member in Florida: "We are structured so that our mission follows the passions of our membership – mission with children's homes, the homeless, ecumenical work with our neighboring congregations, etc. We receive lots of special offerings during the year so we can do more than our budget would allow. We're starting a Drum Circle in November to help reach out to more youth than just our own. We're talking about planning a mission trip for all ages. We have more and more people going to Presbyterian Cursillo and we have several small groups started."

An American Baptist church in a small city provides space for a court-mandated 40-week course for domestic batterers.

From the 19-member Disciples of Christ church in Indiana: "In 1971 this church was formed after a bloody split with the more charismatic arm of one of the oldest Disciples of Christ churches in the country. From its beginning, the life of this congregation has been filled with fights and fights, power struggles, and temper tantrums. I am the 14th pastor to serve this church. Today the church is very small – all of our families, with the exception of our pianist and her husband, were members of the church well before the split. We are older, mostly retired, and we are Anglo. For 30 years we have been known around town as 'that church that fights.' In the last couple of years, however, we have become known by others in our community – others we did not see or even know lived in our community. We are known by the Hispanics in our town as 'the church that teaches English.' In 2002 we were without an organist, and a woman visited us one Sunday and offered to play our piano for us. She was a retired Spanish professor and asked if we'd like to teach an English class for Hispanics in our community. She told us many want to learn English but there are no classes close by. We said yes. Each Thursday evening, 'Survival English' class meets from 7-8:30 p.m. The class is free and children are welcome. We babysit younger children; we tutor older children. 88-year old Dorothy teaches numbers. Linda teaches new students to say, 'My name is ..., my address is..., my phone number is...' Our church members have learned a little Spanish. Spanish is seen in our worship bulletin. We have special bi-lingual services a couple of times a year. Our new friends are always invited and do attend our church suppers. We have been invited and we attend first communions, confirmations, weddings, novenas for the Virgin of Guadalupe. The face of our church is not changed. But, we are changing the face of our community."

A United Church of Canada pastor in Alberta writes: "As minister, I've coined the term 'Small Church, Big Ministry.' Another elder describes us as 'a modern one-room schoolhouse.' We have a small worshiping congregation on Sunday morning – yet our multi-purpose building is busy throughout the week. We have a strong ministry of adult faith studies, often planned around a meal that gets commuters home to bed early. We have a labyrinth ministry and recently started a spirituality program for those with dementia.

Our building also houses the local Food Bank, literacy programs for parents and preschoolers, mother's morning drop-in, Scouting and Guiding groups, a support group for families who have experienced violence, and a grief program for children. We consider these partners in ministry – not simply user groups – and are intentional about working with agencies that fit our mission and values."

A Mennonite church in Indiana says: "Five years ago we revitalized our young adult Sunday school class and invited college students from a nearby college to a weekly fellowship meal hosted by rotating groups in the congregation. Since then we have served as a home congregation to over twenty college students who have attended regularly (not all simultaneously) and enriched our worship and fellowship. Two have chosen to become members. A monthly prayer and Bible study at the local retirement center is especially appreciated by those whose health does not permit them to attend worship regularly. A Barnabas Minister program matches volunteers from the congregation with someone in the congregation or community who they visit regularly. A monthly support group works at sustainable lifestyle issues. Another small intergenerational group does regular water quality testing at the river as part of the Hoosier Riverwatch program. (One reason for our interest in the nearby river is that we regularly hold baptismal services there.)"

Eight years ago a Lutheran congregation in Florida started a hospital hospitality house in an old building next to the sanctuary. This has become a community ministry where they provide housing to patients who come into town to go to the research hospital. The same congregation opened a nursery for working mother coming off welfare in conjunction with a local social service agency.

The Rector of an Episcopal church in Florida shares these thoughts on outreach: " I have had the experience of meeting new people who find out I serve at [this] church and reply with things like, 'Oh, that's the church where people who aren't sure they want to go to church go.' In other words, we are especially gifted as a warm, welcoming, accessible, and inclusive church, and often baptize adults new to the faith. We attract a diversity of people: rich and poor, Buddhist and Jewish, married couples with young children, gays and lesbians, young adults and wealthy elders living in retirement communities, chefs and surfers, maids and at-home mothers, influential newspaper publishers, architects, attorneys, and physicians as well as underpaid and at-risk people."

The pastor of a Missionary Baptist Church in North Carolina writes: "We formed our Partnership Ministry that cuts across denominations and church cultures. Our Partnership Ministry can be divided into two areas. First there are our local partners who we join together with in bringing biblical direction to daily issues in our local community. Second there are our outreach partners who we work with on national and international mission projects. [One] local project of the Partnership Ministry has been our covenant partner relationship in the Stop the Funeral Initiative. After the senseless death of two young people in our community, over 38 churches, ministries, and businesses came together to address the violent deaths among young people in our community. [Our church] was one of the initial covenant partners providing financial support, personal leadership, and spiritual assistance to the group and citizens affected by violence.

From an American Baptist church member in Vermont: "Our congregation is aging. We have far more over 50s than under 50s. All of us seem to work well together, but we are VERY busy. We have started to think of our church as a 'missional church.' The congregation is committed to discovery. We are becoming a 'go to' for community organizations as a place for housing 501(c)3 organizations, providing space for workshops, etc. We see this as our unique ministry in our own town, as we have an ample amount of space in our building. So we share (or give space) to other organizations such as AA and an organization committed to eliminating domestic violence, and we are in the works of starting a Free Clinic with the support of a local retired doctor and local funding."

An urban Disciples of Christ church in Washington State with a building that takes up most of a city block: "We are a small congregation of mostly older persons. What makes us unique is the commitment among the congregation. We offer several different ministries of hospitality: an Advent noon concert series, housing the emergency overflow homeless shelter for two weeks, hosting a Thanksgiving dinner for the community. In 2007 we hosted a tent city for homeless persons for 90 days; this year we will be hosting them again – with help from our neighboring synagogue. "We have discovered our greatest gift is hospitality. When we open our doors and hearts – to persons who are hungry, homeless, and those who long for beauty – we grow and receive gifts. We are opening ourselves to persons who are among the 'least of these.' In return we are gifted by our guests' presence. During the tent city in 2007 we met Ani and Randy. They became engaged while the tent city was with us. Several of us attended their wedding in the spring. This summer my husband and I visited them at their workplaces [in another state] and saw them thriving. Now back in Washington for two months, they recently volunteered at our emergency overflow homeless shelter! They are giving back. Their lives have blossomed and we are privileged to be part of it. What a blessing!"

7

PASTOR AND PEOPLE

LEADERSHIP

Leadership in Family and Pastoral Churches

As we have seen, and as you know from your experience, small congregations are different than larger ones. There are different problems, but also different joys. In his article for *Leading Ideas* entitled "Who is Visiting Small Churches These Days?" Lewis A. Parks identifies five types of persons who keep showing up as visitors to small congregations:

- Persons seeking surrogate family.

- Persons seeking an alternative to the anonymity of the work place and public square.

- Persons weary of self-absorption and in search of a corporate story into which they can jump.

- Persons who have a score to settle with God but want to settle it in a safe environment.

- Persons who are looking for a place to give back for the blessings they have received.[41]

It makes sense, doesn't it, given what we know about the nature of the small church. I doubt if any of those reasons would draw someone to a large church and keep them there, except perhaps the last one. There is a lot of promise in the context of our nation and our post-modern culture for the small congregation to thrive. The key is realistic, authentic, relational, healthy leadership.

> Think of the real purposes of any church: to worship God, to grow in knowledge of God and the human situation, to provide resources to support Christ's kingdom and to minister to church members, the community and the world in the name of Christ. Small churches perform these vital functions as well as big churches do and frequently much better. On average in a small church the attendance at worship represents a much higher percentage of the membership, the stewardship is better per member, the instruction is in smaller groups and may therefore be more effective, and leadership development is much better because there isn't pressure to function on a "professional" level.[42]

It is essential to life in a healthy small church that there are healthy, effective leaders. However, the leadership qualities desired in the small church are much different than in larger churches. It is much more important for leaders in the small church to be relational than it is to be business-like. Value is held not as much in getting the job done as in making sure everyone is on board and comfortable with what is being done. A pastor who comes into a small congregation with the attitude of "this is what we are doing, and if some people don't like it, they can find someplace else to worship" will find that the web of relationships in the small church are tight and complicated, and offending one person might cause half of the congregation to leave.

Pastoral leadership and lay leadership in small congregations require more of a servant's attitude than in any other kind of ministry. Putting one's own needs in the background in order to seek the good of the group is a skill that must be learned and practiced. This is not to say that a pastor cannot accomplish anything in the small church, but it must be handled carefully and over time. Coming in like a fiery bull with a set of agenda items will result in being ignored or sabotaged, or worse.

History is important in the small church – leaders must learn the history of the church so they can understand today's context. Some event from the past that was tried and failed may be fresh in the minds of parishioners (who have LONG memories!) and even though it seems like a perfectly good idea for today, that history will win out and cause the congregation to prepare for failure again.

Pastors must be in tune with the culture of the church or churches they serve – each congregation is different. Laypeople who grumble about the other church in their cluster are simply not understanding that the culture of that church is different from theirs. Pastors and lay leaders alike must learn that there is no universal formula for success in the church. Libraries are full of books written on "how to" grow your church, or increase your Sunday School attendance, or do mission, but they are useless in the small church outside of its context.

Change is notoriously difficult for small congregations, but it is not impossible. Significant change can occur in small congregations when relationships are valued, history is valued, cultural context is valued, and it is taken slowly. In some small congregations it takes the shock of realizing that their beloved church may close in order for members to accept the fact that change must happen. This surprise often occurs after years and years of decline, and often comes too late. They have been told by pastor after pastor, but until someone has invested the time and relational energy into developing trust, they will not believe it. Still, leaders must be visionaries. They must envision the future, while respecting the past and the present. It takes great skill to be able to put the brakes on ideas in order for the people to catch up.

Lovett H. Weems, Jr., professor of church leadership at Wesley Theological Seminary, talks about small church leaders living "in the middle," in the tension between a vision of the future and the reality of the present.

> This tension is inherent if the leader becomes the steward of God's vision for the congregation. One cannot give in to the current reality and abandon the vision to which God is calling the church. Nor can one simply lift up the vision and ignore the realities. To be a leader means to stay with the tension. It also means to stay with the people. Remember, people in the small membership church are often people who are living on the edge – geographically, economically, theologically, and culturally. They know whether you are living with them or not.[43]

He goes on to say that clergy and lay leaders in small congregations must be bearers of hope to a people who may have lost hope. We, as followers of Jesus Christ, must be able to share the message of hope not only with the members and friends of our congregations, but with those in our workplaces, our communities, and the world. Hope begins in faith, and faith comes from telling our story. Leaders in the church must be reminders and encouragers of the faith we have, "so that we may be mutually encouraged by each other's faith, both yours and mine" (Romans 1:12). It is this hope and encouragement that gives us the freedom to try new things and put our faith into action, both inside and outside our small congregations.

The Pastor Shouldn't Be the First One at the Church on Sunday Morning: Lay Leadership in the Small Church

One of the most important and potentially most difficult aspects of ministry in the small congregation is the development and nurture of lay leaders. Churches in which the pastor is happy to defer to the needs, ideas, and abilities of the people are healthier churches. There is no place for unhealthy ego issues among clergy in the small church.

Churches with strong lay participation and leadership are more vital. One of the biggest frustrations I hear from small church pastors is "they expect me to do everything." Some of this is certainly due to complacency (or busyness) on the part of the people, but some of it might be due to the clergy person's attitude – it's easier to do it myself; it'll be done right if I do it myself. Empowering lay people to ministry does take a lot of time and energy on the part of the pastor, but isn't that what ministry is about?

In visiting small congregations, it was always a good sign when I pulled into the church parking lot with the pastor on Sunday morning and there were already several cars there – people setting up chairs, or checking the pews to make sure everything was neat and tidy, the kitchen abuzz with coffee-makers and folks setting out snacks, the choir rehearsing. This told me that the congregation was not so dependent on its pastor that nothing could happen until he/she got there. In the overwhelming majority of churches I visited, it was the case that the doors were unlocked, the coffee was on, and the lay people were making "church" happen. In fewer cases, but still the majority, the pastor was not the last one to leave, either. Teams were set up to lock up the church, make sure lights were off and clean-up was done, and reset the tables in the Fellowship Hall for the aerobics class that meets on Mondays.

The idea of the laity as "co-owners" of the ministry (with God, not with the pastor) is a new one for the church, and is counter-cultural. Although we live in a democratic society, in most cases we still expect our leaders to make decisions for us. They are the paid professionals, so we assume they have the knowledge and the wisdom to best run the organization. It is easy and natural to entrust all of the power in the leader, but in the church, especially the small church, it is different. If there is no buy-in on the part of the laity, if they are merely performing tasks to please the leader, there is no church. Churches of all sizes and types who are completely dependent upon the vision and drive of the pastor have experienced complete disarray, loss of members, loss of vision, and loss of ministry. In healthy small churches, the laity direct the ministry. The pastor is there to empower and encourage and equip the laity, and to offer professional guidance when needed.

I know there are some who will disagree with the previous statement, and certainly in some denominations the polity seems to direct clergy to be more in-charge than this, but the nature of the small church is such that even in hierarchical denominations there is no value in having a minister who is a dictator and the laity as the peasants who carry out the will of the leader. Clergy who enter into ministry in the small church with a need to be in control are probably going to be less than successful, or, if the congregation does follow blindly, the ministry will be less effective at touching lives and making disciples.

In a 2009 article in *Presbyterians Today* magazine, the author tells about two small congregations who have made the intentional decision to "embark on life without installed pastoral leadership." They rely on supply preachers to perform those duties only pastors can perform (in the PCUSA that is the administration of the sacraments), but do mission and ministry in their communities by themselves, or with lay pastoral leadership. And the churches are thriving in communities that are not experiencing growth.[44] This may not be the most desired model, but it is one that makes disciples!

Effective lay ministry does not happen by itself, though. It takes hard work on the part of the pastor to train, encourage, support, and celebrate the ministry of the laity. Clergy and church leaders can work on a lay ministry plan to build up the gifts and talents and passions of the members and friends of the church, and can all work together to implement that plan. "The mission of a church is enhanced when people work together. Leaders in the church, members of the congregation, and people in the community will benefit from your hard work and dedication to discipleship when you develop a healthy lay ministry.[45]

Julia Kuhn Wallace, formerly of the United Methodist Church Small Church office, offers the following list of considerations for those recruiting lay leadership:

- Take the time. Understand the leadership roles the congregation has identified as vital to ministry. Use that understanding to discern the qualities and special characteristics needed to successfully fulfill the role.

- Pray. Consideration of leadership is never a forced decision or putting someone on the spot, but is a matter of prayer when discerning people to ask, and during the asking process.

- List potential leadership. List and investigate all "leads," even those who might not seem like likely choices.

- Visit and invite! Without using desperation techniques or stalking or guilt trips, simply call people you want to invite to consider leadership and ask when you can visit to discuss service in the church. Make an appointment, then visit, don't call on the phone or email. Thoroughly explain the position and what it entails. Give them time to think and pray about making the commitment.

- Check back! Remember that an honest "no" is better than a half-hearted "yes." Thank them for considering the opportunity, no matter what their decision.

- Support the person. Move beyond "yes ... thank you" to "yes ... you can depend on us." Leaders need encouragement and training. The job of lay leadership isn't finished when you have your leadership list filled. Stay in contact with the persons you invited to serve and make sure their time of service is a positive, growing one.[46]

Equipping and Supporting Lay Leaders

The pastor can't do everything, and shouldn't do everything. Lay people who are involved in ministry and mission will be more committed to the life of the church, will increase in discipleship, will be more excited about telling others about their church, and will be more fulfilled. For clergy, the goal of ministry should be empowering, equipping, and encouraging the saints – the lay members and friends of the church (Eph 4:12-13). To begin this process, spend some time with the leaders of the church (matriarchs, patriarchs, board members) to identify and recognize the spiritual gifts of all of the members and friends of the church. There are various denominational resources for gifts assessment, but be careful to try and find one that is realistic and relevant. Or, develop your own based on a few available tools. One I developed is included in Appendix I of this book.

Although gifts surveys can be valuable and eye-opening to those who participate, there are other ways to identify persons to ask for particular tasks. Resist the temptation to publish general pleas in your newsletter: "We need Sunday School teachers! Please help us out by calling ..." Not only are these types of pleas ineffective, they can be dangerous. People want to be asked personally, based on particular gifts you see in them for a specific job. "Mary, I noticed you seem to enjoy the children in our church, and you have a great way of communicating Bible stories when you lead the children's message during worship. Would you consider co-teaching the 3rd through 6th grade Sunday School class for the next quarter, along with Jim, who has been doing it for awhile and would like to take a break next year?

We'll be having a teacher training workshop at church in two weeks." By using this approach, you have noted personal things about Mary, you have offered her a co-teacher to help her get started, and you have shown that the church will support her with training events. Much different and more effective than the "cattle call" approach.

Get to know people in the congregation and find out where their interests lie. Offer training for activities like teachers, lay readers, ushers, and chalice bearer, etc. Co-lead an adult education class and then turn it over to a layperson for the next round. Begin a class to empower those who are gifted to do pastoral care (one useful program is Stephen Ministry, but it can be expensive!). Give people small jobs that will build up confidence for larger jobs. Honor "no" when someone says it, but ask again in a year or so.

Don't assume professional teachers want to be Sunday School teachers, and bankers want to be treasurers. Those people may have other gifts they'd like to try out, and would rather not continue their professional life on Sunday at church.

Train your church council members to be more than placeholders at the monthly meeting, more than members of the board of directors. Remind and encourage them that they are the spiritual leaders of the church. Engage in a monthly book study, devotion, or other exercise that will aid in discerning God's will for the church. Some helpful resources building up the ministry of church leaders are:

- *Transforming Church Boards into Communities of Spiritual Leaders,* by Charles M. Olsen

- *Discerning God's Will Together,* by Danny E. Morris and Charles M. Olsen

- *Transforming Vocation,* by Sam Portaro

- *Living on the Border of the Holy: Renewing the Priesthood of All,* by L. William Countryman

- *Hearing God's Call: Ways of Discernment for Laity and Clergy,* by Ben Campbell Johnson

- *Becoming a Blessed Church,* by Graham N. Standish

Promote a climate of trust and openness in the congregation. This starts with the clergy, and in small congregations, it may take some time to achieve this. Many small churches suffer from pastors who have stayed too long, pastors who have not stayed long enough, pastors who were sent to a small church because they messed up in a larger church, new pastors who come in with unrealistic expectations and no real training in small church, bad interim pastors, and so forth. Many of the people in these congregations have been hurt by these pastors, so trusting a new pastor is difficult. This should be a primary goal of the new pastor in a small church – being trustworthy and developing a culture of openness.

When the pastor has a good idea, it is essential that she/he get a group of lay leaders to help develop it. For one thing, it will give you a support group when you are ready to present it to the congregation. For another, the Holy Spirit works through other people beside clergy! The nature of collaboration is that the original idea and vision might be radically changed by the group, but it is often better than the original and is "owned" by the lay leadership. Those presenting ideas might find that their original idea is very different in the end, but it is better and is "owned" by the lay leadership.

Finally, affirm people who do anything – you can't say thank you enough! Give children a chance to try something in church (like playing an instrument or taking up the offering) that they wouldn't be asked to do at school or other places, and affirm them, even if it's not done smoothly or professionally. Recognize teachers and behind-the-scenes workers during worship. Some congregations have an annual "appreciation day," where all volunteers are recognized. Others incorporate it into the prayers each week, mentioning a different role in the life of the congregation.

Just like clergy, lay leaders can be healthy or unhealthy. Some of the signs of healthy lay leaders, and the antithesis of health, are:

- They confront and cope with the situation in which they find themselves with confidence and purposefulness. Antithesis: complaints about being too small, too isolated, too old, etc.
- They rejoice in relating to different types of people and experiences, knowing that in this Jesus Christ can make a new creation in His church. Antithesis:

they're not like us, so we don't really want them here (they may change us), or, we've never done it that way before.

- They trust the connectional system of the church and/or denomination, and see its value. Antithesis: no one can tell us what to do in OUR church.

- They bear witness to God as revealed through Jesus Christ in the midst of the world where they are. Antithesis: the church as a social gathering; it is not inclusive; it is not aware of its surroundings and the changes in the community.

- They risk the commitment and suffering necessary for the mission of Christ and His church. Antithesis: this has worked for the past 150 years, it should still work; or, we're too old to change.

- They have a hopeful and optimistic view of the future which grows out of their assurance of God's presence known to them in Jesus Christ. Antithesis: everyone here is over 70; we'll just die out.

- They laugh and cause others to laugh. Antithesis: what is there to be happy about?[47]

The Importance of Spiritual Leadership

The one thing that distinguishes a church from a community helping organization is very basic – it is the reason we are who we are and do what we do. It is our love of Christ and our desire to serve him and serve the Kingdom of God in this world. While this is simple, it is a struggle for many small congregations. The goal of ministry ought to be the transformation of lives, but in fact we often spend all of our energy "keeping the trains running on time," and doing creative budgeting such that we sometimes forget why we are here. In some congregations, you can barely tell what makes them a church: the "worship" service is filled with loud rock music that sounds more like love songs than praise to God; the message is a string of jokes and humorous stories designed to keep us awake; there is a feeling of getting-through the liturgy so we can move on to coffee hour and gossiping about others. There is no discernable mission or ministry, and council meetings are indistinguishable from business meetings.

As with everything else in the small church today, I think we need to get back to basics. We need to remember why we are gathered and what our mission is. Leaders in the church must understand the mission of the church, and seek to carry it out. The church members and especially the leaders need to be able to articulate their spiritual identity. The church generally and the small church particularly is counter-cultural; I see this as one of our greatest strengths. Otherwise, why would someone choose to attend a church instead of the gym or a bar or a book group? But individuals in the church, and especially its leaders, must be able and willing to be different if we are to present a viable alternative to those seeking faith and fulfillment.

Part of the way we do this is in giving people the language they need to articulate their spirituality. Much of the modeling of that comes from the leadership. Are all meetings opened with prayer? Are committee members encouraged to seek the will of God rather than their own interests? Leaders should reflect on their own spiritual journeys and the spiritual journey of the church with questions such as:

- Why did you begin going to church?

- What keeps you here?

- What are some ways you have developed your spiritual life?

- What can this church do to support you in your spiritual journey?

- How is prayer a part of your life?

- How do you experience God's call to you personally?

- What tools can the church provide to help you to read the Bible regularly?

- Tell about a time when your faith made a difference.

- How can hospitality/mission/fellowship/education/evangelism be changed from tasks to spiritual practices?

- How can we be most attuned to God's will as we make decisions?

- What do you think God's hopes and dreams are for this congregation?

- How do you experience this congregation as a spiritual place?

Sometimes the language we use and the way our attention is focused can make all the difference in the spiritual life of leaders and congregations. I often tell churches, especially when speaking to the leaders, how Graham Standish, in his book *Becoming a Blessed Church* takes time during a meeting where decisions are being made to seek the will of God. Instead of asking the group to respond to "all in favor say aye," he asks, "all who believe this is the will of God, say aye."[48] "When I tell them this, the reaction is always the same: a gasp from the church leaders." And then, a thoughtful, "hmmm, that would really make a difference." I hope some of them tried it, and incorporated that slight language change into their meetings.

The example of spirituality in a church comes from its leadership. Leaders, including the pastor, must be willing to read the Bible on a regular basis, pray, seek God's will, respond to crises with faith, and be spiritually alive and in touch people. Obviously this is a lifelong process, but one that many churches sadly ignore. If we believe in the power of God through Jesus Christ, we must be willing to walk that walk along with preaching and teaching about it. You might be reluctant to change your habits if your overweight, chain-smoking, alcoholic physician admonished you to get healthy. The example church leaders set for character, behavior, and attitude is vitally important to the spiritual health of a congregation. The qualifications for church leaders in 1 Timothy 3 are a good place to start when choosing leaders, and when looking at personal disciplines.

> The most important quality of pastoral or lay leadership in a church is character. It's not enough to ask someone to serve in a leadership role because of his or her education, status, talents, or how long he or she has been a member of the church. Character is more than moral or ethical behavior, although it certainly includes these qualities. It also has to do with whether a person is seeking to live his or her life in accordance with God's will. Spiritual leaders are persons who are growing in their faith.[49]

Stewardship and Other Unpleasant Subjects

Stewardship season is that time of the year, usually in the fall because it's harvest time, when we beg for money to keep the church going. No one likes to do it. Clergy hate it because it seems so self-serving (trying to raise money to pay their salary); congregation members hate it because it seems like all the church ever talks about is money (even though it was one of Jesus' most talked-about subjects). Treasurers and finance committee people hate it because there's so much stress involved in collecting pledges and working out the budget, or in the case of churches who don't do pledge cards, guessing at what the giving will be. So if everyone hates it, why do we do it? Well, the church is supported through the giving of its people. In order to pay the pastor, we need money. In order to keep the lights on, we need money. And so on and so forth. So we NEED money, and we try to convince people to give and give a lot. Right?

What if we looked at stewardship from a spiritual point of view? The spiritual practice of stewardship begins with hearing the Good News of Jesus Christ. It is the power of the Holy Spirit working through Word and Sacrament that changes our hearts and wills so that we become the generous children of God. The practice of stewardship continues by providing opportunities for people to live out their faithful and joyful response to the Good News of Jesus. It's not just about giving money to a budget or giving our time to teach Sunday School. Stewardship is a statement of faith, a declaration of trust, an act of hope, and a thank-you note to God.

The question in stewardship needs to be moved from "How do we raise enough money to pay the bills for the next year?" to "How can we further the mission of Jesus Christ in this church?" And the behavior of people in the church shows that the emphasis on the spiritual side of stewardship is more effective than the fundraising side. People in small churches tend to give to vision that they can get behind. Many a struggling small church will attest to the fact that although members moan and groan about the economy when they are paying their pledge, if someone in the community experiences a tragedy, they are the first ones there with open wallets. They have the money to give, in many cases, but lack the motivation. Wouldn't you rather contribute money to something that helps a fellow human being than to a new hot water heater for the church?

A long time ago, when I was a new church elder chairing the Stewardship Committee, the theme for stewardship that the denomination proposed to congregations was "Responding to God's Grace." That was a life-changing phrase for me. It takes money out of the mix for stewardship. It makes percentages and tithes and even needs into tools to decide how much to give, and gets to the important matter of faithfulness and thanksgiving. When giving becomes a response to what God has already given us through Jesus Christ, we cannot be generous enough!

Spiritual leaders in the church should set the example of stewardship as a spiritual discipline. If someone is not giving to the church, particularly its leaders, there may be something amiss with his or her soul, and perhaps pastoral care is needed. During a difficult time in my life, when finances were very tight and I was a single mother with two daughters to raise, I was unable to keep up my pledge to the church, and I will say it really damaged my spirit. I missed that joy of giving mentioned in 2 Corinthians 9:7.

During the lean financial times our country is facing, talking about giving money and even giving time and talent are challenging. People are working multiple jobs to make ends meet. The people we want most in the small church are young adults with children, who have the least disposable income of just about any group in the church. Perhaps we need to give permission to our church members to respond to God's grace with whatever means they can at this time in their lives. Perhaps the stay-at-home mom is more able to give volunteer time during the week while the kids are at school than a hefty check on Sundays. Maybe the out-of-work business person can offer classes in writing resumes to others who are out of work.

Stewardship is about managing responsibly all the gifts God has given to us. And don't forget to teach stewardship to children. They have gifts and talents for ministry too. If an offering is collected in Sunday School, collect it be for something that the children can connect with, such as food for hungry children or help for people who have lost their homes in a flood.

Some suggestions for small churches and stewardship:

- Put a face on financial needs – invite people inside and outside the church to tell stories of how mission dollars are used.

- Be creative in fundraising, and don't do it too often. Involve the community by holding an annual dinner or picnic that attracts a lot of attention. Find ways to get the local media to cover your event.

- Celebrate strides being made in the church, due to the generosity of people. There cannot be enough partying in a small congregation!

- Small churches are about relationships. Encourage members and friends of the church to share their stories of how God has made a difference to them.

- When talking about stewardship, include things other than money. Let the congregation know that the pews will need refinishing this year, and you may have someone come forward and volunteer to do it for the cost of materials. One church planning to open a preschool ministry registered with the local Target store as if the church were having a new baby. They registered for the items they needed, and to their surprise they received gifts from people in the community. They held a baby shower and had a couple of pregnant women from the town open the gifts. They not only received their preschool and nursery supplies, but also made community partners.

- Ask church leaders to be the first in line when asking for pledges or special offerings.

- Praise the members of the church (including leaders) for their generosity. Keep things positive![50]

Leadership, both clergy and lay, is vital to the health and well-being of the small congregation. Careful, intelligent, compassionate leadership can help the congregation to weather the tough times and find their identity as the people of God.

Below are some examples of effective leadership (and frustrations) in the small churches I have visited.

The pastor of a Lutheran Church in Iowa writes: Our ministry

together during the last six years has been a struggle. [Our church] is a church that has had frequent changes in pastors in its 150-year history (I am pastor number 41). This constant change of clergy and a few distinct, brash personalities had created an atmosphere of friction. The congregation was not used to connecting with their pastor to develop a relationship of trust and guidance. The few strong outspoken personalities provided most of the leadership in the church, and the rest of the congregation remained quiet but often hurt. The church had adapted to a comfortable pattern: the pastor stays a few years and the strong personalities stepped in and relieved the members of any worry or involvement. While the members accepted this pattern, feelings were being hurt and the ministry was ineffectual because of the strong personalities on one hand and the apathy of members on the other. In consultation with the Assistant to the Bishop, I began to name and describe the issues that I experienced. At first only new members could understand what I was saying. Eventually others began to see the pattern and recognize their apathy in the situation. A Spiritual Discernment Team was organized and led by a very talented member who had training in "systems processing." We have written a mission statement, goals, and objectives for ministry. We have entered a program to develop traits that build healthy ministry.

From a tiny United Church of Christ church in the mountains of Colorado: [This church] recently celebrated its 140th anniversary. Over these years, church membership has fluctuated wildly. When the mines still operated, folks tell me the sanctuary was packed. We are far from packed today. [The church] has barely survived for the majority of the past twenty years, many of them without a pastor. We now average 22 on Sunday mornings. Because survival had so long been [the church's] primary occupation, the idea of planning seemed a luxury to the congregation. Early on, I insisted that we begin some mission activity to benefit those in our own town, explaining that we couldn't truly be a church if we didn't care for others. Initially there was resistance ("We can't afford to keep ourselves afloat, let alone..."). Now mission has become such a central focus of who we are that most cannot recall the time (not so long ago) when we had no such activity at all. This past year, I was able to lead my congregation through the first planning process in memory. Our plan includes increasing mission activity in our community and beyond, welcoming all who come to us, offering joyful and diverse worship experiences, dealing openly with controversial issues, and exploring ecumenical opportunities.

A ministry with two United Methodist congregations in South Carolina that each have fewer than 20 in attendance on Sunday mornings – "These churches were accustomed to Sunday morning worship only – no outreach, no Bible studies, no social time. Within six weeks of our arrival, 50% of both congregations participated and shared in an eight-week small group study on forgiveness. That led to a second and third small group study, then outreach providing personal hygiene items to a local nursing home, then school supplies to a local elementary school. Then they were asking for more outreach, women's Bible studies, Sunday evening services, monthly socials, women's groups – and especially activities held with both churches in attendance. As they came together for all these functions – yet continued to worship in their 'own' churches – they began to understand a deeper meaning of 'the body of Christ.'"

Leadership sometimes has more to do with the congregation leading toward God's vision than one person's individual leading of a group. Look at the story of a small, primarily African-American Episcopal congregation in South Carolina, a congregation that was formed in 1914 when the local "white" congregation would not allow their servants, who were black, to receive Holy Eucharist, though they were members of that same church. Today the church is mostly African-American, but with a Caucasian pastor. Their rector writes: Three years ago, [our church] participated in a miracle that has profoundly affected us and others who joined us. We had worshipped since 1955 in a small single structure built of concrete block, where the furnishings had to be moved around to accommodate Sunday School, meetings, dinners, and worship in the same space. In 2002, we began to build a new church worship space. But we built it in a new way. The building was constructed Habitat-style, with our own members and those of other Episcopal Churches in our area and diocese coming together each weekend with their own particular skills. If we couldn't do a task, we prayed for someone who could – and that person always popped up! We had blacks and whites, wealthy and homeless, old and young, conservatives and liberals, charismatics and old-guard Episcopalians getting our hands dirty together. Before we began, we were the "black church." Now we are the "miracle church." On Sundays we are visited often by others who helped us – just so they can see their friends and worship together. Previously they would have been afraid to go to a black church. Now we are faced with "What do we do next?"

A Non-Denominational new church plant in Buffalo, New York: This church took a bold step to move into an older building in Buffalo to be present for the coming revitalization of that area. The church is made up of a dedicated group of families, and has had some success in reaching out to the tenants in our building, many of whom struggle with various addictions and mental illnesses. We sit strategically in an area populated in close proximity by economic extremes of wealth, middle class, and poverty, but all of whom want to be considered Buffalo urbanites committed to city dwelling. In a city predominantly segregated in terms of worship experiences, we have chosen to be in an intentional relationship with another small congregation. Our congregation is primarily African American; the other congregation is primarily White. We worship together every fifth Sunday, each church taking turns to close down their morning service for the merged fellowship. Both congregations have felt strengthened by this fellowship, and continue to explore if this leads to further merging. The vision has always been to establish a vibrant worshipping and service-oriented church that could be a model of interdenominational, intergenerational, interracial, interclass fellowship; a unique city ministry with a specific commitment to using the worship arts as a tool for building disciples and for outreach. This would include a recommitment to interdenominational Bible Study based out of the church, the producing of a gospel musical I wrote about the life of Christ as an outreach tool and re-establishing the church as the home of the urban community orchestra I started some years ago, as well as expansion of our nursing home ministry and 15-year Bahamas church partnership.

One pastor's plan for visioning for her two small Episcopal congregations: In January and February I'm making one hour home visits to each family in each congregation. My questions to each family will be: a) What nurtures you at church? b) What programs/liturgies do you want to participate in during the coming year? c) Are there programs/liturgies that you, personally, don't find as nurturing? d) Are there aspects of what we do as a church that you'd like to see us do more of or less of? e) Is there anything I haven't asked you that you want for me to know? Then in March and April we'll hold cottage meetings (segregated by congregation) to discuss some of the salient issues that will surface from my family meetings. I won't be present for those meetings; Vestry members will facilitate. In May the vestries will meet for a joint vestry retreat, discussing what they learned from the cottage meetings in a plenary session for the first half of the day. The second half of the day will be devoted to the vestries meeting separately to begin to articulate a five-year plan for their respective parishes. They will share their results with one another at the end of the day.

Another United Church of Christ church in rural Idaho relates this story: The church building is situated just around the corner from the high school, which has an open lunch policy on Fridays. Every Friday, the pastor opens the church for teenagers to come and have their lunch. She sits with them and talks with them, but does not proselytize or try to get them to join the church. Her presence with them is enough; if one of those youth has a problem and needs to talk to a pastor, she is the one they will think of.

A United Church of Christ pastor from New York State writes: The congregation supports me in dedicating 15% of my time to UCC Association and Conference work. And they support the work of the UCC with generosity and dedication in financial ways too. Once we were referred to as "the little German church.' We still sing "Silent Night" in German on Christmas Eve, serve homemade sauerbraten at the Harvest Dinner, and celebrate with Faschnacht before Lent. Yet still we are changing, adapting, and becoming more diversified in our membership. We are trying to hold on to the best of what we have and adapt ourselves by bringing in the new that augments and supplements the old. At one time this congregation was of an "either-or" mindset. Now, I have put in place a "Yes-and" disposition. Once it was 'either we do this or do that, not both'; now we say, 'Yes, we can do what we have always done, and we can do something new too.'

From the pastor of a United Methodist Church in New York State: Folks of various ages and backgrounds have been able to appreciate each other's perspectives and pull together toward a greater vision with a sense of adventure. Although there is a tendency to credit the pastor, accomplishments in recent years are a true reflection of the congregation's strengths and potential. I have done nothing more important here than faithfully holding up the mirror so that folks can see themselves more clearly. And they are rightly excited about what they see. In exchange, I have learned much about my own gifts, my faith, and my calling through their reflections back to me. My greatest challenge in my work with this church is to stay fresh and in touch with the Spirit's leadings. There are surely the usual small church challenges of finding common vision, organizational vehicles, resource development, intervention strategies, and increasing self-confidence. All of these things are learnable, manageable, even enjoyable in their adversity when I am leading from an empowered place and able to hear God's voice in the midst of all the others.

The priest in an Episcopal Church in Virginia writes: This family-sized parish had $100,000 set aside for a full-time rector as well as $65,000 for contingency. (They had been saving the money for 15 years for the goal of a full-time rector.) Upon questioning this money, I challenged the parish to consider the reality of calling a full-time rector and how many families it would take to reach that goal. In the end, the congregation voted, almost unanimously, to give the money away. $50,000 was set aside for a domestic violence center in town (which grew to $100,000 for that project) and $30,000 was given to other charities named by the congregation at an open meeting. This was a transformational moment for this church, both for its members and for the community. While they still dream of a full-time rector, our goal working together is to have them to the point where they can at least be in a position to call a part-time rector upon my retirement.

From a pastor in a United Church of Canada cluster in Ontario, which formerly was a five-point parish until the presbytery closed two of the congregations in the late 1960s. She writes: Since then there have been ongoing discussions regarding the need to be one congregation, but no changes. I was appointed as a supply pastor in 2006. At that time the three congregations were deeply divided about being one church, and had experienced several dysfunctional years with the incumbent minister. They were, however, worshipping together in one service on Sunday, rotating location among three buildings on a monthly basis. As I ministered with them I shifted their focus to their relationships with each other instead of just trying to be "one church" – which for them meant one building. On Pentecost Sunday 2009 the three congregations voted unanimously to amalgamate, to amend their governance, adopt a new mission statement, and establish a new name that was inclusive of the area. I was called as their permanent pastor in July of 2009. We are now working on the next step – assessing our physical assets. Looking at our five communities and the local needs and working with the new mission statement, plus being very much aware of the need for accessibility, we are striving to determine the best way to 'house' our ministry. Our congregation is very visible in the community – especially with our Clothing Depot (one of the churches that closed in the 1960s serves as the location for this outreach ministry), a Food Bank ministry, and the number of our members who serve on community-based boards. The follow-up to this story is that two years later the congregation voted to sell all of the buildings and find a new space. This was a momentous decision after 40 years of discussions, but there is a new spirit in the congregation. Much of the reason this finally happened with relatively little conflict was the skillful leadership of the pastor.

A joint United Methodist/United Church of Christ congregation in suburban Seattle: [This church] is the merger of two small struggling congregations in 1970. We have folks from all denominations in our congregation because they have found a welcoming and safe place to be on their spiritual journey. Our one requirement is that folks honor our radical inclusiveness – that there is a place here for you no matter who you are or where you have come from. So we have Republicans and Democrats, military and folks strongly anti-war, lesbian and gay folks, people of color, and spiritual abuse refugees. It is this ministry of radical inclusiveness and welcome and safety that makes us unique as a small congregation. We did a long-term study using Kennon Callahan's Small Strong Congregations and identified this identity as well as our commitment to living our motto "United in Love, United to Serve" as our major strengths. We are a very active, involved group of folks and are known as such in the community.

From a Presbyterian Church in California: [Our church] is a 115-member multi-cultural congregation. We use two languages,

English and Chinese, in our Sunday worship services and in all our Session and committee meetings. I preach in English and I work with a Co-Pastor who preaches in Mandarin. Our style of being together allows for wonderful opportunities for our diverse community to interact and grow into a uniquely diverse Christian community. We see ourselves as a model for being the church for other churches as well as a model of reconciliation in our community.

8

THE FUTURE OF THE SMALL CHURCH

Envisioning the Future of Your Church

In order for small congregations to survive and thrive, we must begin to think differently about ministry. I hope you have seen from the previous chapters that small congregations who get back to basics, examining why they do what they do and setting a clear, relevant mission that involves all people in the congregation will help small churches best use our human and financial resources. Using a positively-focused process like Appreciative Inquiry to get at the congregation's passion will help to connect our desires with God's desires and build self-esteem. Looking at the past but not living in the past can help us to move forward into a new day and a new way of ministry. Listening to the voices of those who are not usually heard can show us where we can make a difference.

When embarking on a visioning process, the first thing to do is to establish the identity of the church. On the board or with the whole congregation, ask yourself these questions:

- What are the things that attracted me to this church when I first visited?

- What things cause me to stay now?

- What are the most important things to us as a congregation?

- Are our values in balance with the Great Commandment – to love God and love neighbor?

- How is our church seen by the community? Do they know we're here? What is our reputation – the church that serves the poor; the church that fights all the time; the church with the wacko pastor; the church that values children?

- How can we let go of our failures and build on our strengths?

Many congregations spend a lot of time writing mission statements. These can be helpful, although many are not. A mission statement should be a very short, concise statement of the overall purpose of the church. A mission statement defines the church's primary objectives. It is used to tell the world who you are and why you are there. Mission statements are often printed in bulletins or on banners in the narthex.

A vision statement also defines the church's purpose, but in terms of its values. It gives direction on what to do next, what our three-to-five year plans are, how we will put life to our mission statement. Its prime function is internal – to define the key measure or measures of the church's success – and its prime audience is the leadership team and the congregation. How do we envision our mission being carried out? With a mission statement, the question is: what are we here for? With a vision statement, the question is, where do we want to go? The vision statement sets the direction for your work.

When writing a vision statement, your mission statement and your core competencies can be a valuable starting point for articulating your values. Be sure when you're creating the vision statement not to fall into the trap of only thinking ahead a year or two. The vision presented may only apply to the next year or two, but the thinking behind it needs to reach further. Once you have a vision statement, it will have a huge influence on decision-making and the way you allocate resources.

When articulating your dreams, make sure you check back with the mission statement to make sure the vision is in line with your purpose. For example, if your mission statement is "to be a witness for Jesus Christ in our community and the world," and your vision statement says, "We will provide pastoral care for members of the church in an emergency," how can you reconcile the two?

Dream your dreams: One way to begin thinking about your vision is to imagine that there is a news byte about the church on the 6:00 news; you are being interviewed. What is it you'd like to be interviewed about? What would you like your church tobe known for in the community?

After you have your vision statement, commit to it. Share it with the congregation – better yet, involve them in setting the vision. Use it when planning your budget and forming your committees. Put it on Board agendas so everyone is looking at it in the course of your business meetings.

It isn't hard to write a vision statement. But it is sometimes difficult to write a vision statement that truly encapsulates the vision for your church. When you write a vision statement, make sure that you have chosen the vision that is most important to you. If you don't fully believe in your vision statement, you won't be able to fully commit to it, and writing a vision statement that you can't or won't fully commit to is a waste of time.

One process for visioning your ministry is to set a list of priorities on a flip-chart. Review the priorities and divide the group into teams based on committees (Christian Education, Outreach, Worship, Building, Fellowship), asking people to be in the group in which they have the highest level of interest (up to 3 or 4 per group) to come up with one or two vision statements for the next five years. Give each team a marker and a piece of flip chart paper to write their statements. Make sure you use the information from the newsprint on what is most important. Coming up with new ideas that the congregation will buy into means honoring the past and being aware of the needs of the community/church members and gifts of the present congregation. Each group presents its ideas to the whole group, which discusses the vision statements (it is best to get affirmations first before the naysayers speak).

By articulating your church's mission and writing vision statements to work out your mission, your small church will have a sense of purpose and a way to check back to make sure you are on the right track. They should be used, not put in a drawer and forgotten. They give a church a way to move forward that does not depend on a strong pastor or a lot of lay persons.

The Changing Role of Clergy

It is becoming more and more rare for a small congregation to be able to afford one full-time pastor of their own. George Bullard says that if a congregation has fewer than about 80 in worship, they probably need a part-time pastor.[51] Herb Miller would say it takes about 125 worshippers to be able to afford a full-time minister.[52] These numbers vary, of course, because of differing resources in churches, differing salary requirements in denominations and regions of the country, and differing educational requirements of clergy. But even if we accept the lower number (and Bullard does acknowledges that seminary education might not be necessary for pastors), that still means that most small congregations cannot afford to call a pastor to a full-time position. Or if they do have a full-time minister, other areas, especially mission, suffer.

In this section we will look at traditional and non-traditional models for ministry for small congregations that your church might consider. Each model has pluses and minuses, so consider carefully before making a decision.

One Church, One Full-Time Pastor

This is the traditional model that most churches would say makes them a "real" church. All of the pastor's time is devoted to that one congregation, which offers a high degree of pastoral care and presence to the congregation. Many small congregations are so sure they need a full-time pastor of their own that a huge portion of their budget is devoted to paying the pastor's salary. Different denominations have stricter requirements for clergy salary packages, but in addition to simply paying the salary, housing must be considered, as well as medical insurance and pension which, in some denominations, can add as much as 35% more to the salary and housing amount. It is not unusual for a small congregation to have a budget of, say, $120,000, and have a clergy salary package total around $80,000.

Obviously that doesn't leave much money for maintaining a building or furthering the ministry and mission of the church. In the best case scenario, a full-time pastor of a small church will spend at least 50% of her time ministering in the community, and the rest of the time attending to matters directly related to the church. By focusing full-time only on the church, amd helping the church begin to grow, the expectation will remain that the pastor will minister at the same level with a higher number of people. Lay ministry can suffer if the pastor is the one paid to do everything, and this may well become a source of frustration with the congregation, especially when the budget gets tight.

One Church, One Part-Time Pastor

This could be an ideal situation for a pastor who is raising a family, or who has other income (such as spouse's income) and does not need full-time work. The cost to the congregation is less, making the budget more balanced and able to support more ministry and mission. The church still has "our own pastor," but the time required more reasonably reflects the needs in a small church. It is hoped that because of the part-time nature of pastoral services, more lay people would be equipped and empowered to do ministry, rather than depending on the pastor for everything.

The downside to a part-time pastorate can be discovered by asking any part-time church professional if there really is such a thing as part-time ministry. I have even heard search committees posit that if they hire someone part-time, the person will probably work full-time anyway. Although this may make economic sense in some businesses, this is the church, and we are called (no, required in Micah 6:6-8) to seek justice for all people, especially those in service to the church. It is up to the congregation (but mostly to the pastor) to make sure that part-time means part-time. Clergy are doing no one any favors if they put in 60 hours when they are being paid for 20 hours a week. How will the person who follows them every be able to put any limits on themselves? How will the congregation grow in discipleship if the pastor is doing everything, and is the only one donating as much or more time than he is being paid for?

Churches should be very clear with the pastor and with the congregation when deciding to call a part-time pastor. Expectations should be clear. Perhaps the search committee can be charged with helping the new pastor to set boundaries.

Two or More Churches, Yoked, With One Pastor

This is usually a full-time position in which the financial responsibilities are shared by more than one congregation. Often, but not always, the ministry and mission are shared by the congregations. Youth groups meet together, mission projects are done as one, sometimes the councils are shared and meet on the same night.

This can be a good situation when there are a number of small congregations in close proximity to one another, and they want to maintain their identity, and usually, their own building. "Place" is very important to many of those in small congregations, and maintaining a building full of memories and history can be a powerful force.

Many times congregations yoke because the distance between the two churches is too great for members of the congregation to drive to one or the other. Then it is the pastor of the yoke who has to do the driving. Scheduling on Sunday morning can become challenging, as the pastor must be at one church for an 8:30 a.m. service, then rush out before adult education begins so that she can make it to the other church in time for worship at 11. A United Methodist pastor in northeastern Minnesota had a two-point charge, one of which was 30 miles from her home going east and the other 30 miles from her home going west. Every Sunday morning she would make the 120-mile circuit – her biggest challenge was finding another pastor to fill in when she wanted a Sunday off! In another yoked ministry, the Lutheran pastor reported that the Council of one congregation met for their monthly meeting while he was off to preach at the other. He felt the situation helped to build up lay ministry in the church, and has only occasionally had to ask that a decision be reconsidered.

Yoked or shared situations can be healthy and helpful in keeping valuable ministry alive, but when the two congregations have very different personalities and the only "yoke" between them is the pastor, it can be a challenge. The churches do not share any ministries, their missions are different, they host separate fellowship events and mission projects, and they may be very different theologically and liturgically. The pastor must make major adjustments to the Sunday morning message in order for it to be meaningful to two such different congregations. This situation doesn't seem as healthy or missional as one in which the churches advertise themselves as "one church in two locations."

Bi-Vocational or Tentmaker Pastors[53]

More and more small-church clergy are opting to be bi-vocational, which allows them to be part-time pastors of a small church while pursuing another vocation, whether secular or not. The bi-vocational pastor, or "tentmaker," has long roots in the Apostle Paul, who would set up shop selling tents to help finance his missionary journeys in the various towns he visited.

Some congregations appreciate a pastor who is "one of us," a working person who understands the challenges of working in the secular world. It certainly allows them to pay less for a pastor, who may be on a health and pension plan through his other employer. Pastors can answer God's call to preach and teach and provide pastoral care in the small church without worrying so much about where the church will get the money to pay the salary. They will have opportunities for connections with unchurched people and with community agencies. Lay leadership can be developed to help in those times the pastor is unable to be there.

Of course, there are limits to this kind of ministry. Bi-vocational pastors are not as available to parishioners as a full-time pastor might be. Some bi-vocational pastors' jobs will not lend themselves to receiving phone calls at work, or to needing to leave in the middle of the day for a pastoral emergency. When a church is looking for a new pastor and considers a bi-vocational situation, it may be difficult for their potential pastor to find other work in the town in which the church is located, necessitating either a long commute for the pastor to her secular job, or a pastor who does not live in town. Bi-vocational pastors must also be masters of self-care and time management if they are to pursue two jobs.

Many find great joy and satisfaction in bi-vocational ministry, however. One Episcopal priest I know felt called to work as a non-stipendiary priest. He grew up in the Deep South, and had never lived anywhere else, although he had a sister in Minnesota. He served a church in Louisiana while working for the Department of Social Services as a social worker. Along the way, he sensed that God was calling him to be a non-stipendiary priest in South Dakota – a real shift from life in the South! He followed God's call there.

As long as the congregation and the pastor are in harmony over expectations, bi-vocational ministry can be an answer to prayer for a small church. It does seems to me that a pastor considering bi-vocational ministry should do some serious self-reflection about whether her or his call is to ministry and their other job is to pay for their call, or whether pastoral ministry is a supplement to their regular job. But I believe bi-vocational ministry will continue to be a viable option for clergy and congregations into the future. "The innovation and practicality of these visionaries can inspire new generations to continue to bring vitality to small churches."[54]

Locally-Trained Pastors

Nearly every mainline denomination has an option for clergy that is a non-seminary-trained, non-ordained pastor. In the Presbyterian Church (U.S.A.)these were formerly Commissioned Lay Pastors, and are now Commissioned Ruling Elders. The United Methodist church has Licensed Local Pastors. The Episcopal Church used to call theirs Canon 9 priests, who were actually ordained to the priesthood, but were not seminary educated.

Locally-traiend pastors are often "home-grown", that is, they have been a part of the local church into which they are called to service. Most are trained in some way by the local denominational office and are assigned to that particular church. Their commission or license is usually not transferrable to another congregation unless they receive special permission and further training. They are often closely supervised by the regional office, and in some cases must prepare detailed reports to that office. In some cases a mentor is assigned to guide them in their ministry.

The reason for this option is that many churches in remote areas simply cannot afford or attract an ordained, seminary-trained pastor because of their location or their inability to pay the denominational minimum salaries. Most locally trianed pastors can perfrom the functions of any ordained pastor, including administration of the sacraments, weddings, funerals, and participation in regional church activities. Congregations often like the option of one of their own becoming their pastor, although there may be the danger of a prophet not being "accepted in the prophet's hometown" (Luke 4:24). This option can provide a regular presence in the pulpit, consistent pastoral care, and steady leadership for a church which might not otherwise have that luxury. This is an option for those who are called to ministry in the church, but cannot stop their lives for three or more years to go to seminary.

When the notion of Commissioned Lay Pastors was brought before the presbytery in which I was serving back in the 1980s, I voted against it. I thought that churches needed seminary-trained pastors – after all, Presbyterians are known for our emphasis on education. I thought this was just a way to skirt the complicated and sometimes cumbersome call system, and pay clergy less money. Since I have been working with small congregations, however, I have seen how important this role is. Some of the most dedicated and effective pastors I have met are locally ordained or commissioned. I still struggle with the justice issue, but most local pastors I know are not in it for the money. Regional councils must be diligent in providing proper educational opportunities and mentoring for locally trained pastors in order for them to be true to the Word of God and able to fulfill, and inspire others toward fulfilling, the Great Commission. I do not recall seminary education to be a requirement for ministry in the early church.

Temporary Pastoral Relationships

When installed pastoral leadership cannot be found for a small church, often temporary pastors are put in place. These might be retired clergy who aren't ready to be completely out of the pulpit yet, or week-to-week preachers who are procured through the regional denominational offices. In some parts of the country there are large numbers of non-parish clergy who work in social service agencies or community help organizations. These folks are often free on Sundays and are willing to preach occasionally. Some temporary pastors might be interim pastors (who may have been an interim pastor in that church for the last decade!).

Temporary pastors are just that – they are temporary. Often they do not reside in the community, and may commute from quite a distance, so they are not available for pastoral care or activities of the church other than those on Sunday morning. Often they do not share a connection with the congregation. Temporary pastors are just that – they are temporary. Often they do not reside in the community, and may commute from quite a distance, so they are not available for pastoral care or activities of the church other than those on Sunday morning. Often they do not share a connection with the congregation. Often churches that rely on temporary pastors are simply in need of a chaplain to maintain their worship on Sunday mornings just a little bit longer. It is difficult to be in ministry and mission when leadership is not committed to the congregation.

Ministers From Other Denominations

Many small congregations rely on a pastor from a different denomination to fill their pulpit, because there are no other ministers available, and they figure any pastor is as good as no pastor.

It is certainly true that some denominations are in partnership with other denominations, i.e., the ELCA and the Episcopal Church, or the PCUSA and the UCC. These pastors can supply pulpits in any of the partner denominations with few complications, and a basic agreement and understanding of one another's theology and polity. More and more, however, I'm seeing Baptist ministers filling Presbyterian pulpits and non-denominational folks filling various denominational pulpits.

I am all for ecumenical partnerships, and I believe they are important to the future of the church. What can get lost when clergy in very different denominations fill each other's pulpits, obviously, is a clear understanding of theology, polity, and connectionalism that is the hallmark of denominations. Whether denominations are relevant, of course, is a discussion for another day. Suffice it to say that if your church chooses to fill its pulpit with a pastor of another, vastly different denomination, it should be cleared through your regional office, and care should be taken to retain the perspectives of the denomination to which you are connected.

Student Pastors and Student Interns

Small churches often employ the temporary services of student pastors to help them when they are without a permanent pastoral presence. The upside to students is that they bring a fresh perspective to a small church, they are usually inexpensive to employ, and the congregation can help nurture new pastors in their calling, showing them what life can be like in the small church. Generally, student pastors are only available for worship on Sunday mornings, so full pastoral support is not possible, but they can provide a steady presence in the pulpit and might be able to help with pastoral care.

The downside of employing a student pastor is that their time is limited every week, and the length of their stay is usually short. They are also usually not authorized to administer the sacraments, so special arrangements must be made. It is essential that quality supervision be provided by the seminary or the regional offices.

Some congregations see themselves as "teaching congregations," welcoming student pastors and interns with the full understanding that they will be short-term. The congregation sees its work with students as part of its mission, and feels that they have something important to offer the educational process of clergy by nurturing them through the experience.

Cooperative Parish[55]

A model of ministry that has gained some momentum in the past several years is the idea of a cooperative parish where a number of small congregations (sometimes anchored by a medium to large congregation) work together led by a board. This board might consist of a couple of ordained clergy, a professional Christian educator, an administrator, a youth specialist, an evangelist, and several lay persons. These folks take turns leading one or more of the congregations in weekly worship, and provide other opportunities for the cluster to work together. The ministry team serves the whole parish, not just one or two churches, so individual congregations do not become dependent on any one staff person.

Cooperative parishes have met with mixed success. Some, such as the Presbyterian MATE (Mission at the Eastward)[56] in Maine, have been active for many years. Others find that dealing with six to fifteen separate congregations is too much for a small staff. Some cooperatives have expanded ecumenically, which opens exciting possibilities.

Merging Churches

The "go-to" position of many denominations with a larger and larger number of small churches, many of which are in close proximity to one another, is to merge them. It seems like a reasonable solution to the so-called problem of so many small churches, but I caution you to proceed very carefully. I am convinced that generally speaking, mergers do not work.

The scenario in most mergers is that two small churches are running out of money and either cannot each afford their full-time pastor, or one larger church is doing okay and a smaller one nearby is struggling. The seeming solution is for the two small churches to merge, or the larger church to absorb the smaller.

The reason mergers don't work is that invariably one of the churches in the merger has to give up more than the other. There is loss of a building or loss of a pastor. And loss leads to resentment of the entity that seems to have lost less.

Mergers are like second marriages. When one new spouse moves into the home of the other, there are often feelings from one spouse that the other is moving into their space, and children from one family feel displaced while those from the other family feel encroached upon. The more successful attempt to merge two households and two families is when both homes are sold and the newly formed family moves into a completely different one. That way, no one feels as if "those people" are moving into "my house." With love and patience, and especially a strong desire to make the marriage work, merging two families together can work, but it takes intentional work and mutual goals for the future together.

It's not that different in the church. When both sides are completely sold on the idea of a merger to further and enhance the mission of both churches, and when neither one has to give up more than the other, there is a chance it will work. If it is impractical to sell both buildings and get a new one, perhaps one church should lose their building and the other their pastor, so the loss is equally felt. If both parties like each other, share the same basic personality, and enter into the merger with a sense of purpose and hope, it might work.

The trouble is that most mergers are entered into because of a lack of something-- usually finances--rather than a desire to join together for the purpose of increasing or enhancing mission and ministry. One situation I know occurred when a congregation's pastor retired and another small congregation nearby suggested a merger. It turned out that church was also struggling and the pastor was being asked to change from full-time to part-time. By merging, he'd be able to keep working full-time. When it was suggested that since that congregation got to keep their pastor, they might consider moving into the other congregation's building, suddenly the idea didn't seem so attractive. There was never a sense of shared mission, only of fixing a problem – for one of the churches. The other one would have lost its pastor and its building, and would have felt like guests at best and interlopers at worst.

Another situation occurred when the diocese decided Church A, an urban African-American church, and Church B, an urban white church, should merge. Church B got to keep their large building, and a new African-American priest was hired for the new church. It sounds like this had possibilities, but there was no pre-merger planning and no shared mission. Church A always felt like tenants in Church B's building. They had to travel farther to get to church, so they usually did not come out for non-Sunday activities. Those in Church A were timid about speaking up, and Church B members were comfortable accepting leadership. The merger failed, but not until Church A's building was sold and they had nowhere to go back to.

Remember, small congregations have an acute sense of place. I once asked an older widow in my congregation for a quote about why she loved our church, so I could put it on the website along with quotes from other members. Her response was, "I don't want you to put this on the website, but I'll tell you. I love this church because when I come here on Sunday morning, I can feel the presence of my late husband sitting in the pew with me." If that church had decided to close their building and "move in" with another church, she would have lost one of her main reasons to go to church: the "communion of saints" she felt with her husband.

Mergers can work; I have witnessed successful mergers, but they must be entered into with the primary purpose of furthering God's mission on earth, not of paying the bills. There must be mutual buy-in and comfort with decisions that are made, and this takes a lot of time. Artifacts from both churches should be preserved and the histories of both congregations retold and celebrated.

These are some models of ministry that can make sense for your congregation; your denomination and imagination may suggest others. Small congregations should explore a number of models when deciding what works best to promote God's mission and ministry.

Leaving a Legacy

A sign of health in the small church is that the members are at least as interested in the future of the church without them as they are with the present. The mission and vision is not only about their comfort or care, but about the generations to come. I witnessed a touching moment in a United church in Canada. One of their outreach activities was a concert, held once a quarter, to showcase for the public the talents of the church members. The evening was well-attended, and ended with a worship service. In one snapshot moment during the worship service, I saw an older man lean down and quietly explain to a young boy (perhaps eight years old) just how to take up the offering. The older man had probably been head usher for years and years, but he saw the importance of passing on the legacy to this young boy, giving him the instruction and confidence he needed. Lovely.

Sometimes the legacy is more difficult than simply passing on the traditions. Sometimes the legacy that is left for the next generation involves facing up to the fact that the church as it is will no longer support ministry and mission as the last remaining members die. In those cases, sad as they may be, the legacy left might be a resurrection of sorts, as the church becomes the new home for a forming fact that the church as it is will no longer support ministry and mission as the last remaining members die. In those cases, sad as they may be, the legacy left might be a resurrection of sorts, as the church becomes the new home for a forming immigrant group or a place for a mission fellowship of young believers to meet.

When congregations close, it can be a life-giving affirmation of the call of God to do a new thing. Through much prayer, an honest look at the future of the church and models for ministry, and discernment of God's will, a congregation might decide that the best thing to do is to cease the present ministry so that new ministry can begin.

Like people, churches have life cycles, beginning strong and moving through stability to decline, and then death. Philip Lotspeich, of the PC(USA) Church Growth and Evangelism office, says that the life cycle of the average church is about

80 years.[57] Of course, the life cycle can be interrupted with new ministry, and the process prolonged, which is why there are so many congregations in this country with histories of more than a century. But closing a church does not have to be an indication of failure; quite the opposite can be true. It depends on openness to the Spirit, and willingness to let go of control.

What is God calling us to do in this place? Many congregations have difficulty praying this question in complete trust that God will provide a clear answer. This is why so many congregations seek to seize control of the decision-making process and force conclusions that seem comforting at the time. Others choose not to choose at all. And some congregations will find themselves praying this question for many months, even several years, until doors to new ministry close, leadership positions go unfilled, the community becomes exhausted, offers are made for their property, or invitations are received to merge or yoke with another parish. How God will answer, no one can say, but prayerfully discerning an answer will yield reward in the end.[58]

When a congregation decides to close, or when it makes a conscious effort to keep the future strong for future generations, the legacy that is left is a faithfulness that will be an example for the generations to come. There is no failure in closing, especially if a congregation allows God to resurrect it into a new and vital ministry.

What Can Denominations Do to Support Small Congregations?

Over the years of the Summer Collegium, and in the years since, there has been a happy, upward trend in denominational support for small congregations. Many denominational offices are beginning to come to terms with the fact that smallchurches are here to stay. Some are offering workshops for small church leaders. Some are able to offer some financial help in the form of loans or grants when a small church is doing something innovative. Some provide pulpit supply when there is no installed pastor.

There is still a long way to go, however. Because of financial and structural pressures on regional denominational offices, in many cases there is still anxiety about growing small churches. Many denominational offices would prefer to just close small churches and support large ones. This puts tremendous pressure on the pastors of these churches. One new Episcopal priest told me that his Bishop told him that if the congregation did not grow by 10 members in the next year, it would be closed. "How can I do creative ministry and take risks when I have this sword hanging over me?" he asked, reasonably. Denominational offices must find ways to support the health of small congregations without making it all about growth in numbers. Instead, take a look at how many members who had drifted away were re-activated this year, and what new ministries were begun; consider how what percentage of the small church's budget went to mission, or what percentage of members attended adult education classes. When those statistics are compared with larger churches, small congregations often come out ahead.

Denominational staff should make an effort to visit small congregations as often as they visit large ones. These connections are vitally important, since many small congregations are a bit suspicious of denominational staff and denominational priorities. Find ways to build bridges with the people from the small church so that when they see denominational staff they don't automatically think they're coming to close the church. Host a regional meeting at a small church with a larger building. Highlight the work of the small church in a regional meeting.

When those denominational events are held, make sure the language is geared to small congregations; remember that 70-80% of all churches are small. I don't know how many times I've heard denominational officials say, "We're a [presbytery, synod, diocese, region, district] of small churches." Then why do so many denominations ignore them? When new pastors come into the region to serve a small church, offer them an experienced coach/mentor to help them through the rough spots. It's much easier to deal with the crises that arise when you are a newly ordained pastorof a small congregation when you know that there is someone outside the church with whom you can vent, and who has experience in these kinds of crises.

When good opportunities come across your desk that might be valuable to a small church pastor in the region, pass them on to those pastors. Find some financial help so they can attend. Then ask them to lead a workshop locally for other small churches based on what they learned.

And finally, advocate for equity in the salaries of clergy. Most small-church pastors are paid significantly less than those in the larger church, and that's just not right. The work is different, but it is not fair to say that large church pastors work harder, or that ministry in the small church is less demanding.

We in the church seem to agree with our culture that big is better and that a minister's worth is determined by how much money he or she produces. This seems to be the logic we use to pay our ministers. Furthermore, we hold those clergy who labor for little in low esteem. Some of our clergy are paid four or five times as much as those who work in rural or small-membership churches. When this uncomfortable fact comes up it is usually justified by saying that the highly paid ones are "more skilled." But what is more demanding than the work of a small-church pastor? To be a "general practitioner" of ministry in such a church means that one must do all the preaching, counseling and visitation, teach the teachers, administer the details of the church and be the [denominational] representative in that community – and more. [59]

These small things can make the difference between a denomination and regional offices being perceived by the congregation as a supportive friend or an enemy out to destroy them.

What Can Seminaries Do to Support Small Congregations?

As guilty as some denominational offices are of ignoring the needs of small congregations, seminaries are just as guilty. It is a rare seminary in any denomination that offers a program of study for those called to ministry in the small church. Most seminaries do not even offer a course in small church ministry on a regular basis. And yet, most of their graduates will begin their ministry, or at some time during their ministry career, serve a small congregation. Why are we reluctant to prepare seminarians for this specialized ministry?

One reason might be that those in seminary do not envision themselves serving a small church. Seminarians are often sent to seminary from medium- to large-sized churches. But that furthers the argument that they need to be taught about the small church that they have never experienced!

Another possibility is the age-old battle in seminaries over the balance between academic education and practical education. Some seminaries believe, with good reason, that three years is barely enough time to teach the biblical languages, homiletics, biblical exegesis, church history, the meaning of the sacraments, and a small dose of pastoral care or Christian education. There just isn't enough time for more practical courses. "We take care of the practical through field education," is the mantra I often hear. This question needs to be continually explored. The ELCA seminaries have made strides by requiring a year-long internship during their seminary course, making it four years instead of two. Union Presbyterian Seminary in Richmond is experimenting with a pre-matriculation program as well as a post-matriculation program for students, both of which have strong distance learning components.

Seminaries should offer at least one course per semester focusing on the special ministry in small congregations. At the very least, seminary professors ought to be required to relate their teaching to ministry in the small church. At Virginia Seminary, the evaluation process for courses includes a question about whether the professor brought in multi-cultural learning; why can't the same be asked about small church connections?

In addition, seminaries can offer remote learning, particularly in continuing education courses, for those who cannot afford to travel to the seminary for classes. Offer a lower-cost Doctor of Ministry degree for those in small churches. Offer discounts on courses, or a scholarship fund for those called to ministry in the education courses, for those who cannot afford to travel to the seminary for classes. Offer a lower-cost Doctor of Ministry degree for those in small churches. Offer discounts on courses, or a scholarship fund for those called to ministry in the small church. Make sure your publicity for events goes not only to the "tall steeple churches," but also to small congregations in the area.

It is vitally important that seminaries and denominations are supportive, not dismissive, and offer assistance, not threats, to small congregations who seek to be healthy and vital. Working in partnership, small congregations will be strengthened for ministry in the 21st century, and will make significant contributions to the "big-C" Church, the church that is most like the church envisioned by Jesus Christ and his early followers.

Can Small Churches Survive?

Perhaps the better question might be, can mid-size and large churches survive? In mainline denominations, the vast majority of churches are small. With droves of people leaving rural areas and moving to cities those percentages will only increase. With the focus of the church changing from an emphasis on buildings to the more biblical model of mission and ministry, the definition of "the church" must change. As more and more people find their faith through loose associations, short-term mission projects, and informal gatherings, counting becomes difficult. This is good news! Counting and numbers have been the bane of existence to small, intimate communities of faith. Carl Dudley has said that denominations should include a category on annual statistical reports called "kindred spirits,"[60] those people who participate in the church on a regular basis, but for whatever reason don't join. I would go one step further and throw those reports out altogether. Numbers are one way to assess growth, but certainly not the only way, and they only measure a particular kind of growth. What about growth in faith, growth in spirituality, growth in giving, growth in mission?

The face of Christianity in America has changed dramatically in the past 50 years. Although denominational fights are nothing new, the church in North America is further threatened by the current wave of consumerism, self-centeredness, competition, and an unstable economy. People today are stressed, and seem to look for relief through working harder, abusive behaviors, and activities that numb the brain. The church has a golden opportunity to bring meaning to lives that have no real meaning, to bring relationships to those who are lonely, to bring hope to those who are in despair, to bring Christ to those who are hurting. The hunger is there. We who believe in the good news of the Gospel of Jesus Christ must find creative ways to share that good news with authenticity and relevance.

In the small church at its best, we offer an anchor in the storm of high-powered lives. We offer connections with people in an intimate way that no other organization in society can provide. At our best, we know that no one kind of church is the "best Christian church," so we take away competitiveness. At our best, we remember the welcome God gave to us when we were welcomed into God's family, and we welcome the stranger, regardless of how different that stranger is from the way our church has always been. Small congregations must look for new ways of doing ministry that depend less on the pastor and more on those with the longest investment in the church – the members and friends. We must get rid of our long-held belief that "if we build it, they will come." We must get outside of those buildings we built during the boom of the church and connect with people who are in need of a word of hope, but don't think the church is the place to fulfill that hope. We must get back to the basics of the message Jesus came to give us: love God, and love your neighbor as yourself.

Only then will we in the small church be able to fulfill our mission as the place "where everybody knows your name."

ENDNOTES

1. Dudley, Carl S., *Effective Small Churches in the Twenty-first Century* (Nashville: Abingdon Press, 2003), p. 28.

2. See, for example, the article, "Small Churches Still Dominate in the Megachurch Age," by Bob Whitesal at seminary.indwes.edu/WorkArea/DownloadAsset.aspx?id=220.

3. Routhage, Arlin J., *Sizing Up a Congregation for New Member Ministry* (Education for Mission and Ministry Office by Seabury Professional Services, 1983).

4. Rothauge, p. 5.

5. Dudley, p. 40.

6. Rothauge, p. 5.

7. Ibid.

8. Mann, Alice, *The In-Between Church* (The Alban Institute, 1998).

9. Dudley, p. 10.

10. http://222.barna.org/barna-update/article/12-faithspirituality/289-how-faith-varies-by-church-size, accessed 3/3/2011.

11. National Congregations Study: http://www.soc.duke.edu/natcong/

12. "Special Report: The American Church in Crisis," from the Missional Church Network:http://missionalchurchnetwork.blogspot.com/2007/10/american-church-in-crisis.html

13. Dudley, p. 87-88.

14. Callahan, Kennon L. *Small, Strong Congregations* (San Francisco: Jossey-Bass, 2000), p. 34 ff.

15. Branson, Mark Lau. *Memories, Hopes, and Conversations* (Herndon, VA: The Alban Institute, 2004), p. 24 ff.

16. Branson, p. 137.

17. In my very informal survey of about 90 mainline Christian seminaries, only about 10% offered any course in small church ministry. Some offered courses in rural ministry or urban ministry, and some instructors took a class session in the semester to talk about small churches, but the offerings are few and far between.

18. "God of Our Fathers," Words: Daniel Roberts, 1876. Music: George Warren, 1888.

19. "God of the Sparrow," Words and Music: Jaroslav J. Vajda, 1983.

20. *The Constitution of the Presbyterian Church (U.S.A.), Part II, The Book of Order, 2011-2013.* (Office of the General Assembly, Presbyterian Church (U.S.A.), 2011), W-1.1001.

21. Long, Thomas G. *Beyond the Worship Wars* (The Alban Institute, 2001), p. 53.

22. GIA Publications, www.giamusic.com. I'd recommend starting with "We Walk His Way."

23. Bush, Peter and Christine O'Reilly. *Where 20 or 30 are Gathered* (Herndon, VA: The Alban Institute, 2006), p. 34.

24. "What if Starbucks Marketed Like a Church? A Parable." http://www.youtube.com/watch?v=D7_dZTrjw9I

25. Woolever, Cynthia and Deborah Bruce in *Where 20 or 30 are Gathered*, p. 39.

26. Griggs, Donald L. and Judy McKay Walter. *Christian Education in the Small Church* (Valley Forge, PA: Judson Press, 1988), p. 12

27. A notable exception to the bad children's sermon books is a series of three books by Brant D. Baker, beginning with *Let the Children Come* (Augsburg, 1991), and followed by *Play that Preaches* (Augsburg, 1993), and *Welcoming the Children* (Augsburg, 1995). These are not object lesson books, but experiential ways to involve children in the sermon. They're old and not easy to find, but well worth the time looking!

28. www.godlyplay.org

29. www.rotation.org

30. www.logosproductions.com

31. (Birmingham, AL: Religious Education Press, 1990).

32. www.chalicepress.com

33. There are four volumes in this series by Paula J. Carlson: *Listening for God: Contemporary Literature and the Life of Faith* (Minneapolis: Augsburg Fortress, 1999)

34. Dudley, p. 53-54.

35. Ibid., p. 81-82.

36. Byassee, Jason. *The Gifts of the Small Church* (Nashville: Abingdon, 2010), p. 39-40.

37. www.episcopalcredo.org; www.presbyteriancredo.org;

38. One resource for this is a study by the Institute for American Church Growth, which cites 79% of people say they "came to Christ and this church" because they were invited by a friend or relative. See http://www.visitthecrossing.com/resources/messages/pdf/20101003.pdf.

39. Bickers, Dennis. *The Healthy Small Church* (Kansas City: Beacon Hill Press, 2005), p. 117.

40. From Dudley's keynote address at the Summer Collegium, June 22, 2006.

41. Parks, Lewis A., "Who is Visiting Small Churches These Days?" in *Leading Ideas*, September 24, 2008.

42. Parvin, Ralph S., "The Lure of Upward Mobility," in *Religion Online*, www.religion-online.org/showarticle.asp?title=758, accessed 4/21/2006.

43. Weems, Lovett H., Jr. "Leadership and the Small Membership Church," in *Leading Ideas*, December 6, 2006, accessed 12/6/06.

44. Bolt, John A., "No Pastor? No Problem," in *Presbyterians Today*, June 2009, accessed 6/9/2009 at www.pcusa.org/today/cover.htm.

45. Wallace, Julia Kuhn. "More Pointers on Lay Leadership Selection," from the General Board of Discipleship of the United Methodist Church, http://www.gbod.org/TextOnly.asp?item_id12800, accessed 7/26/2007.

46. Ibid.

47. Adapted from "Pastor and Parishioner Health: Indicators for Effective Ministry," by Rene O. Bideaux for the Hinton Rural Life Center's Models for Ministry.

48. Standish, N. Graham, *Becoming a Blessed Church: Forming a Church of Spiritual Purpose, Presence and Power* (Bethesda, MD: The Alban Institute, 2004), p. 202.

49. Ibid., Bickers, pp. 79-70.

50. Adapted from "Stewardship for Small Churches," by Julia Kuhn Wallace. http://www.christianitytoday.com/bcl/areas/stewardship/articles/021306.html, accessed 4/21/2006.

51. Bullard, George. "George Bullard's Posterous" blog, http://bullardjournal.posterous.com/how-many-staff-persons-should-a-congregation. Bullard is a prolific writer on church growth and evangelism.

52. Miller, Herb. "How Much Staff is Enough?" in *The Parish Paper*, www.theparishpaper.com, Nov. 2005.

53. For a full treatment of bi-vocational ministry, see Dennis Bickers, *The Healthy Small Church* (Kansas City: Beacon Hill Press, 1995), or Bob LaRochelle, *Part-Time Pastor, Full-Time Church* (Pilgrim Press, 2010).

54. Lowery, James L., Jr. "The Tentmaker Tradition," in *The Living Church*, March 26, 2006.

55. For more see Waldkoenig, Gilson A.C. and William Avery, *Cooperating Congregations: Portraits of Mission Strategies* (Bethesda, MD: The Alban Institute, 1999).

56. www.missionattheeastward.org

57. From a workshop at the Presbyterian Center in Louisville, KY, 2011.

58. Spencer, Keith, "Assessing Congregational Viability," in *Ending with Hope: A Resource for Closing Congregations*, edited by Beth Ann Gaede (Bethesda, MD: The Alban Institute, 2002).

59. Ibid, Parvin, Ralph S.,

60. Dudley, p. 64.